SERMONS TO CHILDREN

THE LITERARY REMAINS
OF THE REV.
SIMEON SINGER

SERMONS TO
CHILDREN

Selected and Edited by
ISRAEL ABRAHAMS

With an Appreciation by
LILY H. MONTAGU

LONDON
GEORGE ROUTLEDGE & SONS LIMITED
NEW YORK : BLOCH PUBLISHING CO
1908

PREFACE

MR. SINGER seems to have been among the first to make a regular feature of sermons for children in an English Synagogue. Long before the introduction of special services for the young, he chose the Sabbath immediately following each festival for sermons meant for children. Later on he appropriated the seventh days of Passover and Tabernacles for the purpose.

In these talks to children the preacher was admittedly at his best. Children looked forward with delight to the occasions on which Mr. Singer was expected to address them. His knowledge of the child mind, its foibles and strength, his rich yet simple humour, his inexhaustible store of apt illustration, his love for and belief in the young, combined to make him an effective preacher to them. And his adult hearers enjoyed the sermons quite as much as the children did.

His own views as to the composition of children's sermons are shown in the sermons themselves. It may be of interest, however, to insert here some notes of a lecture delivered by him to the Homiletic Class at Jews' College. These notes are printed as they were taken down by one of those present on that occasion. They do not represent all that he said, but they are a faithful record of the substance of some of his remarks.

Sermons to children may serve two purposes. They affect the older members of the congregation, for grown-ups prefer to be exhorted *indirectly* ; when they know that the sermon is not primarily intended for them, they are the more likely to take it to heart. Children, on the other hand, love to think that the sermon is meant for them. Unlike adults, children are best got at *directly*, they are put upon their mettle, they listen with all their ears, and they are most inspiring listeners. They sometimes answer your rhetorical questions ; I like to hear them do so, but I never lay traps for this effect consciously.

The subjects chosen must be simple, the text short if possible, and something they can easily remember. The preacher's language must, of course, be simple. It is absurd, however, to suppose that " simple " language is identical with " baby " language. Some classes of children naturally have read more than others, live in more cultured homes. But you can be quite unintelligible to *any* class of children, even though you use the most easy words, if your ideas and treatment are hard. You will avoid certain hard words, but on the whole it is best to use the *right* words, sometimes long words ; have no superstitious dread of them. You can interpret the words if necessary. Let your ideas be simply conceived ; let the thought be within the child's compass ; the language will more or less take care of itself. It is a fundamental mistake to do as some preachers do, and write as they would for adults, and then go through the manuscript and alter harder words into easier ones of one syllable. They have not thereby made themselves intelligible to children.

Avoid metaphors, or rather translate them into parables. Story-telling is absolutely essential, but it is not enough in itself. You must always have a high religious object in view. Your anecdotes must have a pertinent application. You may make the children laugh, there is no harm in that, but you must turn the laugh to serious account.

Do children like satire ? I fear that I am sometimes too given to the sarcastic tone with them. Do not follow my example. Children are sensitive to ridicule, and are very uncomfortable when laughed at. It may be a good or a bad thing to make them uncomfortable. The question is, I take it, not, Do they like satire ? but, Does satire profit them ? It will not profit them if it be unjust. Never charge children with faults from which they are free. Never be bitter. Appeal to their sympathies, their affections, above all to their sense of honour.   Touch their charity through their own happiness, get them to share their happiness with the less fortunate.

Be concrete.   Ask them for definite sacrifices, definite services. Send them home with some specific good intention.   Cure a definite fault, encourage a definite virtue.

Never be too long, and above all never *read* your sermons to children.   They cannot follow you if you are looking at your paper.   Prepare every word, write it all out, if you find that best, then make short notes and speak from them.   Finally, take thrice as much time over writing a children's sermon as you take over one of your ordinary discourses.

A striking feature of Mr. Singer's sermons for children is their frequent illustration from natural history. Despite his urban upbringing, he was a devoted lover of nature.   He had far more than a superficial knowledge of science.   He revelled in the beauties of the fields and skies ; he loved animals.   And what he possessed by instinct and gained from observation he cultivated and rendered precise by reading and by constant visits to the Natural History Museum, Kew, and the Zoological Gardens.   Nothing gave him greater satisfaction than the scientific bent and distinction of his son Charles, and a good part of the illustrations in this volume were the actual results of talks and studies between father and son.   And, later on, he found a peculiar delight in taking his young granddaughters to the " Bird Museum," as one of them named the noble institution in the Cromwell Road.   Whenever he visited Cambridge he would be met at the station by the children, and would proceed at once to the University Botanical Gardens.   Thus there was about his sermons to children a freshness as though nature herself had inspired them.

Many, but by no means all, of his children's sermons ended with a prayer.   Only a few prayers are printed in this volume, for Mr. Singer did not often write them

out.   He did, in fact, write in full many of these sermons,
but he never took the manuscript into the pulpit.   He
followed the method which he himself describes, and
actually preached from notes on half-sheets of letter-
paper.   He mostly succeeded in getting his young
auditors to join in the prayers.   He would ask them
to repeat the words after him, and by his skilful phrasing
made it quite easy for the children to follow.   Thus in
1897 he officiated at a Thanksgiving Service attended
by 1,300 children at the Great Synagogue, London.   In
a published report of the proceedings we are told that,
" After his address Mr. Singer called upon the children
to rise in their places, put their hands together, close
their eyes, and repeat after him a prayer of thanksgiving
which he gave out to them.   The recital of this English
prayer, in which all the children joined, was the most
impressive feature of the service " (*Jewish Chronicle*,
October 29, 1897).   Mr. Singer composed many prayers
for the young, among them one a Morning Prayer, for use
at the Parkwood Recreation Home.   Here will only
be cited one instance.

PRAYER BEFORE RELIGION LESSON

Almighty God, who hast promised that those who seek Thee
earnestly shall find Thee, be with us this day and every day.
Send forth Thy light and Thy truth that they may lead us.
Bless all our efforts to understand Thy will and to study Thy
word.   Help us, we beseech Thee, during the days of our youth
to refuse the evil and choose the good.   And as we grow in
years and bodily strength, so also may we grow in wisdom and
goodness, in the love of truth and honour, in gratitude to Thee
our heavenly Father, and in lovingkindness to all Thy creatures.

The thanksgiving sermon, alluded to above, differed
from Mr. Singer's usual addresses to children.   In his

own congregation, the children's sermons were delivered at the ordinary morning service, and were intended for older as well as younger children in the presence of adults. But the gathering at the Great Synagogue was a special service for children only. He had a firm belief in the necessity of such special services, and at the time of his death was occupied in preparing an adaptation from his Prayer-book for the use of children's services on the New Year and Day of Atonement. In his own congregation, he cordially supported Miss Lily H. Montagu in her successful resolve to establish weekly services for children in the Vestry Room. He often officiated at these services. So, too, he wrote several sermons for use at children's services in the East End of London, though he was not able to deliver them himself. One thing he maintained. Children's services must be services for children, not services for adults cut short. There is a plausible objection against this view. Being mainly in English, and thus unlike the synagogue service, the children's service is not a preparation for the synagogue ritual. But though plausible, the objection is not altogether conclusive. With reference to his own scheme for special services for young women, he answered the same objection in the following way. He said that no one wished more than he to encourage Hebrew, but he could not allow the hearts of those to be starved who could only pray in English. " It is a good thing to encourage swimming. But shall the lifeboat refuse to save the drowning, lest people might think they need not learn to swim ? " In the case of children it is found in practice that those who begin to acquire the praying habit at the children's services are the keenest to attend the

adult services as they grow older. " Let them learn
to pray, and the language will take care of itself." And,
of course, all well-arranged children's services do contain
in Hebrew some of the most important paragraphs of
the traditional ritual.

Above the importance of speaking to children, Mr.
Singer placed the duty of teaching them. Before he
became a minister he was a teacher, and when he became
the one he remained the other as well. He had many
private pupils, but our present remarks will be confined
to his public teaching. In the Borough he took a life-
long interest in the Jewish School, and he was much
gratified when his son David undertook the Honorary
Secretaryship of the same institution. In St. Petersburg
Place he regarded his Religion Class as the most useful
field for his ministrations. He gradually evolved a
unique system which, as the Rev. J. F. Stern said in
his memorial sermon on Mr. Singer, it is to be feared
has died with him. Membership of his religion class
was not limited to the children of his own congregation.
No pupil was admitted under the age of twelve, and
as a general rule, the pupils were older. No pupil was
enrolled who did not solemnly undertake to attend
regularly for the full course of three years. The course
was divided into three parts. Though the course
formed a systematic whole, each year's work was so
far independent that the course could be taken up in
any of the three years. The great difficulty, in the
case of such a course, is the taking of notes. Without
notes little is remembered ; but if the pupil is thinking
chiefly of note-taking, the lesson is not followed with
undivided attention to its subject. Mr. Singer's method
was to dictate the notes : i.e., to give out certain out-

lines, consisting chiefly of clear, terse and precise state-
ments. These were taken down. The pupil was
expected to keep another note-book in which to expand
at home from memory these dictated paragraphs. Mr.
Singer used no one text-book, but quoted from several.
He assisted Mr. N. S. Joseph in the revision of his excellent
volume, *Religion, Natural and Revealed*, for the recently
published new edition. Dr. Friedländer, who always
examined Mr. Singer's class, found the work of the
pupils very efficient. " The teacher's fervour and
enthusiasm had a good effect on the minds of his pupils,
who loved and adored their master. I had frequent
occasion to notice the spirit which animated his pupils,
and to admire the intelligent way in which they discussed
the principles of our holy religion." No part of the
splendid Memorial which his congregants and other
friends have raised to his name would have given him
greater delight than that originated and established
by his pupils.

He also from time to time arranged regular courses
of instruction for adults. Thus in 1898 we find classes
for the study of Hebrew in active progress, and these
adult meetings continued for considerable periods, and
were often revived after intervals. At the special
request of the members he also held classes for the
consideration of the relations between Judaism and
Christianity. He also lectured on the subject several
times under the auspices of the Jewish Study Society.
He would not assent to the view that Jews and Jewesses
can be saved from temptations by closing their ears or
by imposing artificial bonds of loyalty. Justifying
his frank treatment of these topics, he said—

In the old Grecian story of Ulysses it is related that when he sailed past the island of sirens he listened for a moment to the sorcerers' music, and thereupon to prevent himself and crew from being lured to the shore, he stopped their ears with wax and had himself tied to the mast of the ship. Thus, as the story goes, they passed in safety the fatal strand. But when Orpheus in search of the Golden Fleece went by the same coast, he, being a masterly musician, set up better music than that of the sirens, and so enchanted the crew that without the use of thongs or wax they all sailed past the dangerous isle.

In the voyage of life, from childhood to old age, we are exposed to temptations, allurements, perils. One way of escaping them is to force people by restrictions of all kinds, by shutting them out from the world, and making them deaf to its entice-ments, to force them to avoid evil. The system, even when it answers, is an inferior one at the best. In the education of the young, constant and galling restraint does not produce satisfactory results. There is a better way. We must set up better music. We must in our religious training not ignore evil but must guard against the power and attraction of evil by making good more powerful and attractive—we must show forth the majesty of duty, the beauty of holiness, the bliss of faith and hope and righteousness and mercy, the dignity of loyalty, and thus protect the adolescent against the call of lower and alien ideals.

He often preached on the subject of the religious dangers accruing from Jewish boys being allowed to attend Chapel at the public schools. He sometimes succeeded in obtaining the sanction of school authorities for relaxation of rules which interfered with the religion of Jewish pupils. In one important case he found the authorities quite ready to concede an arrangement of marks which would remove the hardship of penalizing Jewish boys who did not attend school on Saturdays. " As far as we are concerned," wrote the headmaster, " no boy shall have to fear losing marks who does work, compatible with his religious observances, and arranged by the masters, presentable on the Monday

morning." It was Mr. Singer who, in the heat of the
Progressive attack on Diggleism at the School Board,
secured from the leader of the attack (Mr. Lyulph
Stanley), an undertaking, ever since honourably fulfilled,
that the class-rooms of the ordinary elementary schools
should continue to be rented to the Jewish Religious
Education Board after school hours. In many other
ways he championed the cause of Jewish children. He
took a leading part in the scheme for providing for the
orphaned survivors of the Russian pogroms. He was
a good friend to the Jewish Boys' and Girls' Clubs,
and bore an active part in the work of the Lads' Brigade
(he was himself Chaplain of the Jews' Free School
Corps). An important service of his was rendered
when, in June, 1898, there met what the *Jewish Chronicle*
described as " unquestionably one of the best organized
gatherings of English Jews assembled in recent years."
This was the Conference on Jewish Elementary Education originated and organized by Mr. Singer with the
co-operation of his wife.

He constantly urged the cause of the Jewish Religious
Education Board. He was fond of the extant denomi-
national schools, acting as regular examiner at the
Westminster Jews' Free School and the Norwood
Orphanage. But he realized that it was futile to expect
that the community would erect new Jewish schools.
In one of his sermons he referred to the demand for a
Roman Catholic University, and went on : " We Jews
make no such request. We are only too glad to have
the old and once most exclusive seats of learning open
to our children. We are only too happy that no distinction whatever is made between Christian and Jewish
children in the rate-supported elementary schools.

All the stronger, however, is the obligation devolving upon the community as a whole to take care that not a single Jewish child shall lack instruction in the sacred language and in the faith of Israel. What our energies are saved in diffuseness they should gain in intensity." Proudly he declared that the Jews of England had a worthy record in this regard. In a memorial sermon, delivered at the Jews' Infant School in 1888, soon after the death of the beloved headmistress, Miss Marian Harris, he said : " Before school boards were thought of, before the state had awakened to a sense of its loftiest functions in relation to those from whom it expects rational obedience and patriotic service, this school was called into being for the benefit of children of the tenderest age, who until then had hardly been deemed worthy of any special consideration." And he described Miss Harris' love for the children of the school and her influence over them, and then he pronounced the memorable sentence, " The glory of a higher than physical motherhood rested upon her." He went on to address the teachers : " Do not approach your task in the spirit of the hireling. No wage of gold and silver can repay your work when well and faithfully done. God is the true paymaster of those who teach the poor. But He will have faithful work if He have any."

The Hon Lily H. Montagu has written an appreciation of Mr. Singer, which is printed on the next page as a supplement to this Preface. It is worthy of the subject, and of the writer. It adds to the beauty of this volume, for it expresses, regarding a true preacher to children, the thoughts of one who is herself gifted with a unique power to inspire the young, and fill their souls with noble ideals.

AN APPRECIATION
BY LILY H. MONTAGU

As one of Mr. Singer's pupils, as one who for many years derived inspiration from his faith, his optimism, his geniality, I would try to write a word of appreciation of our dear friend as a preacher to children. But the difficulty of my task overwhelms me.

I ask myself what made Mr. Singer so beloved by boys and girls of all ages and sections in the community—by tiny children in the nursery, and by old folks in their studies, who were still blessed with the hearts of children ? What was it which made us all certain of his sympathy even before he addressed a word to us ? What was it, that during his address, made us forget our own smallness and insufficiency, our own little trials and difficulties and think the world the best possible place for the average person who did his best ? Was it his geniality, his love of fun, his supreme tact, his living faith ? Was it his power to see the best in everybody and the fun in most things ? I think all these qualities helped to give Mr. Singer's personality the magnetic influence which we all recognized. We remember well how he usually started his children's sermons with a homely story—often funny enough to rouse a titter among the children. Our friend seemed to believe that in a soil warmed by the rays of joyousness he could best plant the seeds of faith. He wanted to put us in a good temper, and when he had us there, he did what he liked with us. He took us into his confidence, asked us to consider with him the moral lesson underlying the homely story. He did not seek his examples in worlds with which we were unfamiliar. He told us about the relation of religion to every-day life, and after his sermon we carried away something which we found again in our homes or in our schools and even in our playgrounds, and reminded us of our friend and his wishes for us.

I remember distinctly as a very young child asking God to make me what Mr. Singer wanted me to be. I felt confident that my teacher cared about me, not as a member of the congregation of children, a unit in a large aggregate, but as myself, in my home, that he knew and cared about what I did and tried to be. It was this feeling of personal interest which made every boy and girl in his own Synagogue, in his own class room, in the classes which he examined and to which he spoke occasionally, determined that it was worth while doing their best. Mr. Singer understood our difficulties, but he expected us to extricate ourselves ; he knew our opportunities, and he meant us to make the most of them. He gave us love and we returned the gift in generous measure, as children will. We knew that Mr. Singer could be indignant, and we respected him for that quality. We liked to hear him speak angrily to certain classes of people, and we determined not to belong to these classes if we could help it. We knew that he hated snobbishness and meanness and cowardice ; above all he despised the boy or girl who was not proud of belonging to the Jewish brother-

hood. His glowing enthusiasm for Judaism increased
our loyalty. When towards the end of his addresses
he struck a note of solemn appeal, asking us gently,
persuasively, certain of our sympathy, to consecrate
our lives to God's service, fitting ourselves by obedience
to our parents and teachers, by our devotion to Jewish
teaching, to bear our part in the grown-up world, we
felt we *could* not disappoint our friend who trusted us
so completely.

I remember passing through the dreary period of life
when my " child's faith " disappeared, and in agonizing
travail of spirit I sought for the God who for a while
was hidden from me ; it seemed to me, as it seems to
all boys and girls before their souls awaken to realize
the meaning of a living faith, that doubts were the
only realities in life, that faith would never return to
me, that it was not meant for me, perhaps (alas for
the arrogance !) that I had risen superior to it. Never-
theless, I was very miserable and restless, and the
days dragged heavily. It was then that Mr. Singer
came to me, as he came to the boys and girls who
attended his religion class during this most critical
period of their lives, and told me that the doubts and
struggles and griefs were normal and useful. He told
me that he was quite confident of the existence of God,
and that he was not afraid to live or die—just as God
willed—because this life was in God's hands. He told
me that he was glad I was seeking for myself a religion
that would suit my own soul. *He* could only tell me
of the one which suited his life, and he could only
show me the lines on which to direct my search—the
lines sanctified by the devotion and sacrifices of my
Fathers. Then he must leave the rest to me. He

knew that I must find the peace I sought; he *knew* the struggles; he had experienced them himself and he knew that they led to peace. This confidence, this sympathy, this optimism, this faith, this tolerance characterized our friend's teaching. We believed him because his personality made us love him. It was the power of his personality and not any special quality in his sermons which made his preaching and teaching a formative influence in the lives of his pupils. It is the recollection of this personality which fills us to-day with hope and gratitude; we know that it will remain with us for ever.

CONTENTS

CLEAN HANDS AND PURE HEART

(*New West End Synagogue,
The 7th day of Passover, April 27th, 1894.*)

PSALM xxiv. 3–6 : " Who may ascend the mountain of the Lord ? And who may stand in His holy place ? He that hath clean hands and a pure heart ; who hath not set his desire upon vanity, and hath not sworn deceitfully. He shall receive a blessing from the Lord, and righteousness from the God of his salvation. This is the generation of them that seek Thy face, (O God of) Jacob."

MY DEAR YOUNG FRIENDS,—There is a story told of a little boy who—remarkable to tell—was seen to wash his hands a great many times on the same day, and—what is still more remarkable—without being told to do so. He had a brother who was not given that way, and the other's conduct roused his curiosity very much. " Why do you wash your hands so often ? " said he to his brother. " Because I want to be strong," was the reply. " Do you think that washing your hands will make you strong ? " " I do." " How do you prove it ? " " Oh, it says so in the Bible ! " " Where ? " The brother took the Bible, and turned to the 9th verse of the 17th chapter of Job, and there, sure enough, it was written : " He that hath clean hands shall be stronger and stronger."

Now, many a worse explanation has been given of a Bible text by many an older person, and I have no hesita-

S.C.   1   B

tion in telling my young friends here assembled and any others whom it may concern, that they cannot go far wrong if they try, first of all, to understand words like these in quite a literal sense, exactly as they are written. " He that hath clean hands *shall* be stronger and stronger." There is no doubt about it ; if you want to be strong, you must be healthy, and if you want to be healthy, you must be clean. These are no trifles. God wishes us to be strong and healthy, and therefore tells us, through his trusted servants, to be clean. Nay more, the text with which I began says : " Who shall go up to the mount of the Lord ? "—that is, who is fit to come before God in prayer ?—Only such a one as " hath clean hands." No one would think of coming into the presence of a human king to ask a favour of him with hands other than clean. How then shall we be so bold as to come before the King of kings otherwise than with clean hands ? And that is why at the entrance to every synagogue there is always a place and water for washing one's hands. In former times water was not, like it is now, laid on to every one's house ; and therefore it was put at the door of the synagogue, so that no one should have any excuse for entering there with dirty hands. It is not, as I have sometimes had to tell inquirers, anything like holy water, nor has it been specially blessed. Among Jews all water is holy and blessed that washes one clean.

But I must not leave you under the impression that there is no more in these words than was imagined by that excellent youth who washed himself so repeatedly in order that he might become strong. The Bible speaks in human language—it would be of no use to us if it spoke in any other. The hands are the instruments, the tools with which men act, and they therefore stand very often for the actions themselves. When Job says, " He that hath clean hands shall be stronger and stronger," he wishes us to understand that if our actions are clean and just and honourable, we shall grow in power to resist evil, and be able to do more and more good. And what the Psalmist, thinking of God's holy place and those who wish to go there, meant to say was, that those are dearest to God who strive to be pure, who have clean hands, and are pure in heart, and do not set their desires on vanity, and do not swear deceitfully ; in other words, those who are pure in thought, in desire, in speech, and in action. So also we read in another Psalm, " I will wash mine hands in innocency," that is, " I will only do such actions as are innocent and godly," and then " I will surround Thine altar, O Lord." The man who wrote these words had a soul which told him that, the purer and the more innocent we are, the nearer we shall feel ourselves to God, and the nearer we shall feel God to be to us.

That is the reason why God is often nearer to young children than to grown up men and women ; for, though their little hands are not always as clean as they might be, their little hearts are mostly pure, and their actions innocent ; and that is the chief matter after all. And God so loves their simple, spotless innocence that, if they die as children, He makes of their spirits the sweetest, loveliest flowers that bloom in Paradise.

However, not all are thus early taken from earth and rooted in Heaven. God thinks of us, who are grown up, also. He gives us little children for our happiness ; and indeed, so long as they are innocent and unstained by sin, they are the most beloved of all our possessions and make up our chiefest blessing on earth.

But years roll on. And as children become acquainted with the world, and grow in the knowledge of good and evil, it is no easy task for them to remain pure in heart and clean in deed. Now, bear well in mind that a pure heart, like clean hands, can only be kept thus by constant cleansing. The more you neglect it, the harder you will find the work of making it pure, until at last the task may become quite impossible. Surely no boy or girl would be so foolish as to argue that because their hands are clean on a holy day, like this, they can afford to let them be filthy afterwards. Much more foolish are they who think that because they do a holy act in coming into God's house to-day, they need not trouble themselves to enter there again for ever so long ; or because for once in the way they have denied themselves some pleasure in order to do good to others, or on some one occasion have been steadfast when tempted to say or do an evil thing, therefore they need think no more and care no more about these things. The heart needs attention not less, but far more than the body. For by neglecting it, it becomes not only impure, but hard. There is a river near Quito, in South America, whose waters have the power of gradually turning into stone any wood or leaves that are placed in it for any length of time. So is it with the human heart ; leave it for a while in the stream of worldly or impure desires, and it will become hard and stony.

Think of what happened with Pharaoh, of whom we read so much during this Festival. When first he began to treat our fathers so cruelly, he could only have done so by wilfully hardening his heart. After a while his heart became hard, spite of himself. It is true that here and there it is also said that God hardened Pharaoh's heart. But God hardened it only in the sense in which He who made the rivers hardens any substance you choose to put into those waters of which I just spoke to you. You are not bound to leave it there, and Pharaoh was not bound to steep his heart in cruelty. Only when once he had commenced to treat the Israelites in an inhuman fashion, and after he had continued acting in this way for some time, he found it too difficult for him to alter his conduct. And so the heart which he wilfully hardened at first became more and more stony as he went on.

Now you will perhaps remember that when I last talked to you from this place I told you of a way in which to make and to keep your hearts tender. You were to put by a penny a week out of your pocket-money, to deprive yourselves to that extent of some pleasure in order to help other children, not so fortunate or so happy as yourselves. I am glad to think that very many of my young friends have acted on that advice, and I hope sincerely they will not break in on such an excellent custom. To-day let me point out to you one way, at least, by which you can keep your thoughts and desires, your heart and your actions pure. It is by *prayer*, frequent and devout prayer.

I do not believe it is possible for any person to truly pray and thereupon to sin. If any one should ever tell you that there are people who pray and afterwards do wicked things, don't listen to him. People sometimes *make believe at praying*, and then they sin. No wonder ! But no one can ever lay his soul open before God— which is what prayer means—no one can earnestly beg of God to come into his life and purify it, without feeling the effect of such prayer in what he does afterwards. He *must* be better for it ; his heart and soul *must* be purer.

During prayer you are in God's company, and even when you cease to pray you are the better for having been for a while in company with the Highest ; your spirit is ennobled, and the grace of God goes with you.

And therefore, I say to you, dear children, if you want to keep hands and heart clean, do like the Psalmist ; pray often and fervently. Don't get out of the habit of praying. Don't begin the day without prayer ; don't end the day without praying ; don't enjoy a meal without offering up a few words of prayer.

That is one of the differences between man and beast ; beasts never say grace. When I think of it again, I am not so sure about beasts. Haven't you seen a dog some times *look* " thanks " after you have given him a nice morsel, though he could not *say* " thanks " ? Surely a human being should not be worse than a dog !

If once you drop the habit of prayer it is very difficult indeed to take it on again. Prayer is often broken off in the same way as friendship is broken off. Many a friendship has come to an end like this : you have received, we will suppose, a great many favours from some one, and you have thanked him regularly for them, but the last kindness you received from him you forgot, or were too busy to acknowledge at the moment. A few days pass, and still you have not thought of it. Then when you do remember it, you are rather ashamed of saying anything about the matter, until at last you hardly like to meet, nay, you will go out of your way to avoid meeting—whom ?—your best friend and benefactor, it may be ! So it is exactly with prayer. If you do not pray regularly, you are likely to let the practice drop altogether. Because, if once you interrupt it, you will put it off from day to day, until in the end you will grow uneasy at the thought of meeting your Heavenly Father ; you will actually be ashamed of being caught praying.

Do not imagine, as some children do, that age makes any difference in the need for prayer.   If it does it only makes prayer more necessary : for the older we grow, the more of God's blessings have been ours, and so we ought to thank Him more, while we want more of His help, and, therefore, ought to put our trust more fully in Him.   What an extraordinary remark that was which a little girl was overheard making to her mother the other day !   " Mother," said she, " when shall I be old enough to leave off saying my prayers ? "   She seemed to think, for some reason or other, that prayer was a mark of extreme childhood, or of infancy, like having to eat without a knife, and that when she was old enough to be advanced to the dignity of both knife and fork, she might give up the habit of prayer.   Not so, dear children !   Not until we are old enough to do without all God's gifts, without food and shelter, without loving friends and companions, without health of body and joy of spirit and peace of mind ; not until the hour is come when all power of thinking and feeling has left us, and we can no longer strive to be clean of hands and pure of heart, not until then may we cease to pray !

And the good you can do, young as you are, if you will try to live a clean and pure, that is, a brave, truthful and prayerful life, is much greater than you as yet have any idea of.   In trying to make yourselves better, you will help to make others better, even though you don't know it, and don't think about it.   Just look again at the Psalm from which I have been speaking to you. The Psalmist first asks, " Who may ascend the moun- tain of the Lord ? " that is, who is he that he is dear to

God, and fit to come into God's presence ? And he answers, " He that hath clean hands and a pure heart," and so forth. Such a one, he says, shall receive God's blessing, and shall be helped to become more righteous still. And then he goes on to say, " This is the generation of them that seek after Him, of them that seek Thy face, (O God of) Jacob." You notice here that we begin with the singular, *he*, and end with the plural, " the generation of *them* that seek after Him."

Now to explain this change, let me tell you a story. There was a boy, the son of parents who were not remarkable for cleanliness. They lived among dirty people, in a very dirty neighbourhood. Well, the boy went to school. One day a strange thing happened. Before leaving school, happening to find some soap, and water being at hand, the boy washed himself. He found the operation so pleasant that he repeated it several successive days. Whatever his complexion was when he arrived at school, he went home flesh-coloured. His mother noticed it and was much surprised. After a while she said to herself, " I can't let that boy of mine be cleaner than his mother," and so she washed herself. Then the father came home, opened his eyes, and thought to himself, "What will become of my dignity as head of the family, if I let my wife and child be cleaner than I am ? " And so he washed himself. And the neighbours coming in, and seeing what had occurred, said to themselves they would not be behind these people. And they washed themselves. And so in the course of time the whole district put on quite another face. It was a perfect transformation scene.

Just so is it in our Psalm. One man is steadfast in righteousness : others follow on. Let one be genuinely pure in heart and in conduct, and he not only receives a blessing for himself, but he becomes a source of blessing to others.   He may even bring it about that a whole generation—all those with whom he comes in contact—will become purer and better for his example.   And for this it is not necessary that one should be a full-grown man and woman.   A little child may lead them.   Even " out of the mouths of babes and infants " God has " established strength " for Himself.   May this be your part also, dear children.   And may all your doings and strivings prove in this way a blessing to yourselves and others !

THANKFULNESS

*(New West End Synagogue,
The 7th day of Passover, April 4th, 1896.)*

PSALM cxviii. 1 : " O give thanks unto the Lord, for He is good ; because His loving-kindness endureth for ever."

MY DEAR CHILDREN,—You have all followed this morning, I should be glad to know that you had all joined in, the Song of Moses, the glorious song which Moses and the Israelites sang when they had crossed the Red Sea. You remember they had all to be silent up to a certain point ; " The Lord will fight for you, and ye shall hold your peace," said Moses to them. But when the danger was over, and they stood safe on the further shore, the people could not restrain themselves any longer ; they had to give vent to their pent up feelings ; and men and women burst forth in one of the noblest songs of thanksgiving that has ever poured from human lips.

What did the children do on that occasion ? It is not distinctly said, unless we are to suppose, that, when it is written " Then sang Moses and the children of Israel this song unto the Lord," what is meant is that the boys and girls joined in the chorus. The traditions of our wise men tell us that God was especially glorified on that great day by the praises and thanksgivings of the very infants of the people of Israel. But really it is unnecessary to say what the boys and girls did, because, unless they were very different then from what they are

10

now, they were probably quite the loudest of the whole party. There are no cheers so hearty and ringing as those which boys and girls can give when they are so disposed. We may be sure that they made their voices heard and put their hearts into their voices. Had they not escaped the greatest danger of all ? Their fathers had to toil in slavery, but against their young lives a hunt was always being kept up ; so long as childhood lasted they were not safe from the enemy. Now they had no longer cause to fear at all, and as they were delivered together with their fathers and mothers, you may be certain their gratitude to God was not only loud, but deep and true.

And that is one chief reason why children are still expected even nowadays to take a great part in the Festival of Passover. Without them the Festival would be incomplete, as incomplete as the deliverance from Egypt would have been, if the fathers and mothers had crossed the Red Sea and the little ones had been left behind. But God loved His people too much to treat them thus, and He knew that Hebrew parents loved their children too much to care for liberty for themselves if their children were to remain in slavery. It is not then parents alone, but children also, who have cause for thankfulness on this holy day, and there is not one of them who might not declare, " Ah, Lord, I am Thy servant, the child of Thine handmaid ; Thou hast loosed *my* bonds. I offer unto Thee the sacrifice of thanksgiving."

It is upon this subject of thankfulness that I would like to say a few words to you this morning. If I wanted to judge the character of a child, I should be satisfied to judge it on this point only : Is it a thankful child ? For what does thankfulness mean ? It means honesty, for thankfulness is a way of acknowledging one's debt, and of paying it, and you can't be honest unless you pay your debts. It means love, for to respond to kindnesses done to you is not only a sign of love on your part, it strengthens the very love you feel, just as every time you put out your strength in throwing a ball you not only send the ball where you wish, but you strengthen the muscles of your own arms. It means manners, because the essence of good manners is consideration for the feelings of others, and where is your consideration for the feelings of others if you show yourself ungrateful to them and wound them by any word or act of yours, or—as often happens—by leaving unspoken the words you ought to have spoken and leaving undone the deeds you ought to have done. Therefore, I say, show me a thankful child, and I will hope all things of him ; show me an unthankful child, and I will fear all things from him.

Of human monsters I suppose there are none worse than an ungrateful friend, and especially an ungrateful child. David was once in great distress because of his enemies ; they hated him, they pursued him, they slandered him, they wished him to die, and did their best to take his life ; but all this did not affect him much ; one thing alone unmanned him, it was when he was compelled to say, " Yea, mine own familiar friend in whom I trusted, who did eat of my bread, hath lifted up his heel against me " ; and even that thought, bitter as it was, was as nothing compared with what he suffered through the ingratitude and rebellion of his own son upon whom he had lavished so much of a father's love. There is no doubt about it that " Sharper than a serpent's tooth it is to have a thankless child."

Curiously enough, it is not always the children who

have the most reason to be thankful, that *are* the most thankful. Sometimes, indeed, it happens that those who have reaped the richest harvest of loving-kindness are the most thankless. They get to think that everything belongs to them of right, and if the least whim or humour of theirs is unsatisfied or thwarted, they deem themselves hardly treated, and do not hesitate to say so. If they only had not received so much, they might have been grateful for less; but it almost seems that the more they have the less they appreciate what they have.

Now, when I speak to the boys and girls who usually attend this synagogue for worship, I feel I am speaking to those who have been favoured very greatly and in many ways. How carefully are you guarded from every kind of trouble from your birth upward! What provision is made for your safety! What care is taken of your health! What an amount of thought and labour and money is expended to make your lives happy! Many a household is governed almost entirely by consideration for the needs of the children of the family. I wonder if you are grateful in the measure of your advantages? Or, let me take a single example of God's mercies to you, which, I fancy, the younger as well as the older ones among you will appreciate. I do not want to hurt your feelings, but am I not right in supposing that a very important place in your enjoyment of life is taken up by eating and drinking? Think with what regularity your food is forthcoming. There are three, sometimes four regular meals a day, with occasional light refreshments to fill up the intervals. For every one of you there is enough, and to spare; never have any of you, not being among the children of the poorest, known what hunger, pinching hunger through actual lack of food, is like.   But there is a corresponding blessing, without which the plenty always at hand, thanks to the goodness of God and the loving care of your parents, would only mock you.   You not only can count on good meals, but you come to them generally with good appetites.   There are people whose larders are packed with good things, and whose tables are filled with the choicest viands, but who cannot enjoy them, and who would gladly exchange them all for your appetites.   So you see you are in this matter doubly favoured. I wonder if you are doubly grateful ?   Let me fix this fact upon your minds by three or four lines of poetry, a little altered from the original Scotch dialect, in which they were written.   I quote them in the form in which a great man was fond of impressing them upon his disciples.   If you hear them once, you can hardly forget them.

> Some can eat and have not meat,
> Some have meat and cannot eat,
> But we have meat and we can eat,
>   Therefore the Lord be thankëd.

Very beautiful it is, dear children, to note how thankful some sweet and gracious natures are for the smallest of mercies that fall to their lot.   Things that many of us would scorn are accepted by such as these with a devout cheerfulness that might teach a lesson to us all.   I have read somewhere the story of a little girl whose mother was so poor that she could not afford to buy any bed-coverings for her child.   The winter that year was severe, and the poor woman, who was an ingenious sort of person, hit upon the idea of using a deal board to cover the child's bed with.   One night, when the cold was very biting, the little girl said : " Mother dear, we are well off, than

God, aren't we ? I wonder what the children do whose
parents are too poor to have a board to cover them and
keep them warm and comfortable ! "

And even more beautiful it is if people continue thankful still, when troubles come upon them, when they have
to bear griefs and disappointments when God takes
from them what He has lent them for a while, for God,
you must know, never gives us things outright, He only
lends them to us for a while, and so He can ask for them
back again when He pleases—such loans, for instance,
as money and health and dear friends and loving relations. We cannot expect to keep them for ever, and
even young children are sometimes bidden to say good-
bye to the very blessings which seemed so necessary to
their happiness, and to trust in God, the Father of the
fatherless, and the Helper of the helpless, alone. And if
we give up what God has lent us, without murmuring
against His will, then we shall be like pious Job who,
having nothing left him out of all his former blessings but
the memory of them, said, " The Lord gave ; the Lord
hath taken away ; blessed be the name of the Lord."

Now that sort of blissful resignation is something which
only those enjoy who believe in God, not simply with
their heads but in their hearts. You see, if a person
really believes in God, he cannot be downcast for long ;
he says to himself, This or that puzzles me, this or that
may be almost too hard for me to bear, but God knows
what is best for me. He is " too wise to err, too good to
be unkind." The holy men of Israel always argued
like that. So the sacred poet who wrote our Hallel says,
" When I lift up the cup of salvation, I will call upon the
name of the Lord ; " and " When I find trouble and
sorrow, I will call upon the name of the Lord." The

Talmud tells us of a man whom people used to call by the kindly nickname of Gamzu, Nahum Gamzu, from the Hebrew words Gam zu which mean : "This, too ;" because whatever happened, he was always in the habit of exclaiming, " This, too, is for good." " Nahum Good-again," we should call him. Another's favourite saying was " Whatever God does, is well done." That was the celebrated Rabbi Akiba. He was an extraordinary man. Nothing could cure him of his thankfulness, not even his death, which took place under great cruelty ; he died a martyr for the sake of his religion, and even for that opportunity to show his faith in God he was grateful. On one occasion he had been travelling on a long and tedious journey and was hurrying on to reach a certain village where he hoped to get a friendly reception and a night's shelter. But the inhabitants of the place were an inhospitable set, and he could find no accommodation there. Night was coming on, and he had to take refuge in a neighbouring forest, saying, as he did so, " Whatever God does, is well done." He had with him a lamp, a fowl and a donkey. He lighted the lamp to guide him, but a gust of wind blew it out, and he was left in darkness. " What God does is well done," said Rabbi Akiba again, and he groped his way in the dark as best he could. All at once a wild cat pounced out of a thicket and carried off his bird. " What God does, is well done." Then a lion fell upon his donkey and slew it. " What God does, is well done." On the morrow he went into the village, but a frightful scene met his eyes. Every inhabitant of the place had been massacred. It appears that a murderous band of robbers had made a descent upon it during the night, and had slain every human being they came across. Then he perceived what a fortunate escape he had had. Had he been admitted he would have fallen a victim like the rest, for wicked people have no respect for the good. And as he reflected further, he understood how his other troubles had all been blessings in disguise. If the lamp had remained shining, or the cock had crowed, or the donkey had brayed, his whereabouts would have been betrayed to the brigands, and he would certainly have lost his life. How correctly it all turned out that whatever God had done was well done. True, things do not always turn out quite so neatly or so successfully in the world, but a grateful spirit, just *because* it always believes there is a good side in things, sooner or later finds the good it believes in, and meanwhile it is guided to make the best of the bad side, so that even that does not prove in reality to be as bad as it looked.

Well, dear children, it is this spirit of thankfulness for all things that I want you to cultivate and make your own. The need for it never comes to an end—either in this life or in the next. " Give thanks unto the Lord, for He is good ; because His loving-kindness endureth for *ever*." Don't be grudging with your thanks. Ask yourselves honestly what have you done to deserve so many and such great favours from God and man ? It is through no merit of yours ; it is, so far as you are concerned, an accident. But if you are ungrateful, that will be no accident. Thankfulness is not all a matter of feeling, as some people think. It is also a matter of habit. Never lie down to sleep when the day is done, or rise in the morning after a night's rest, or partake of a meal without some words of thanks to Him who provides for your every want. " Whosoever enjoys aught in this world without blessing God for it, as it were robs

God," say our sages ; and that is so, because to refuse to acknowledge our debt, and to neglect to repay it even by so much as a word of thanks, is not this to rob the Heavenly Giver of the one thing He asks for ? And finally, never excuse yourselves on the ground that you have no time. You have years of time in which to receive and enjoy all the loving-kindnesses of God ; surely you can have no lack of minutes in which to thank Him !

THE WORKER AND HIS WORK

(A sermon delivered before a Congregation of Apprentices of the Board of Guardians, at the Great Synagogue, Sabbath, December 8th, 1900.)

PROVERBS xxii. 29 : " Seest thou a man diligent in his work, he shall stand before kings."

SUCH a man, say our sages in the Midrash, was Joseph, of whom we have just read this afternoon, who, diligent in his work, overcame ill-fortune, envy and calumny, and rose from the dungeon to stand before King Pharaoh. His rise was rapid. At seventeen he left his father's house ; at thirty he was the Vizier of the King of Egypt.

" Seest thou a man diligent in his work, he shall stand before kings." Such a man also was Moses. His rise was slow. It was not until he was eighty that this man, diligent and faithful in his work, whether in defending his persecuted brethren, or in keeping the flock of his father-in-law, patiently abiding at his task, it was not until he was eighty that he became the shepherd of his people, and was called to stand—before whom ? Before the King of kings.

It is concerning faithful, patient, honest, diligent work, that I would speak to you, my dear friends, whom I rejoice to see here in such numbers, and to welcome this Sabbath afternoon.

And for this reason, before all others, I deem it a happiness to meet you. As I look upon this gathering

of youths who have already joined the great army of
workers, in so many and such diverse forms of labour,
I cannot help thinking what vast possibilities of good,
of usefulness, of honourable activity there are in such
an assembly. You and such as you are destined to be
the backbone of the community. You are helping to
rid us of the reproach that is sometimes levelled against
us, that Jews only care for two or three kinds of pursuits,
and that they differ therefore in a most vital respect
from all the peoples among whom they have settled.

You little think, dear lads, how much we trust to you,
how much we hope from you. I seem to see before me
an assembly like that which gathered round Moses when
the tabernacle was being constructed in the wilderness.
There, too, were designers and artizans ; builders,
carpenters, and carvers ; weavers, embroiderers, dyers,
tanners ; workers in precious stones, goldsmiths and
silversmiths, and many others, all of them children of
the House of Israel, so that when the tabernacle stood
complete, with all its vessels and instruments of service,
it was a monument of purely Israelitish skill and
industry. There is no healthier sign of the social state
of a race than when its members betake themselves to
every class of useful occupation, and look upon none
of the interests of mankind as indifferent to them.
This is what you are doing to-day, as your fathers did
in days long gone by, and I fervently pray that, as God's
blessing once rested upon them and their work, so it
may rest upon you and yours.

Now, there are three objects for which a man may
work. The first object is for wages. I am not one
who would condemn another because he thinks of his
wages as a reward for his work. How can I ask you to

do what I do not do myself ? Live we all must, and most of us cannot live unless we are paid for our work. There is nothing to be ashamed of in saying that a fair day's work deserves a day's fair wage.

But there is something else to aim at, besides wages. That is honour. A true worker must take a pride in his work, else he is a mere hireling. He must take a pride in the thing itself, whatever it be, in which he is engaged. He must love to produce a good piece of work, and feel a joy and a satisfaction in what he is producing, I care not what it be, whether it be a good piece of watchmaking or jewellery, of plumbing or engineering, of cabinet work or carpentry or upholstery, of printing, engraving, carving or turning, or a good coat, or a good pair of boots. Do you think all this is mere mechanical work ? Don't allow yourselves to be misled by words and names. Everything is mechanical to a machine ; but you, thank God, are not machines ; for you it is possible to put something of the spirit of an artist into your work. And you become an artist from the moment you take a pride in what you are doing. " Great is work, which glorifies the worker," says the Talmud. But when does work glorify the worker ? When the worker glories in his work.

But there is something else besides wages and glory to be thought of—there is duty. To work because God has ordained it ; because you love to be independent ; because you do not want to be a burden upon the dear ones at home longer than can be helped ; because you feel that you ought rather to lend them a helping hand ; and, since you are daily growing stronger and more capable, would like to ease the lot of those who are daily growing feebler and less able—in a word to work, because the voice of duty calls you—that is the highest, the noblest and the most inspiring motive of all. " Great is work which sets the worker in a glow," which fires him with a love for the duty that has to be done.

But though all this is true, and every worker ought to know that it is true, there are high-minded workers, and there are low-minded workers. And what is the difference between them ?   Simply this : The high-minded worker puts duty first ; and he puts honour next, and he puts payment in the third place.   And the low-minded worker puts pay first, and pay second, and pay third.

To which class will you belong !   The choice rests with you.   But to make a rational choice you must disabuse your minds of a common but a very foolish error.   One sometimes heard people say, Oh, a trade is all very good, but there are trades that don't suit a Jew ; they are not *bekovoud* ; a Jew ought to learn a nice clean trade.   I quite agree, and so I hope do you, that all Jews should learn and follow clean trades.   But what is a clean trade and what is a dirty trade ?   A clean trade is every honest trade that is honestly conducted ; a dirty trade is that which is dishonest in itself or is dishonestly conducted. Look at it in that light, and a blacksmith's may be a perfectly clean trade, while the business of a dealer in gold and diamonds and pearls may be a very filthy one. What do our wise men say ?   " Do something for a living ; go and flay a carcase in the street if need be, and say not, I am too respectable."

That which will tell for or against us is the manner in which our work is done.   If we approach it with the object of doing as little as possible for others, and getting

as much as possible out of them, our work will tell its
own tale, and we shall sooner or later find out that even
as a matter of business we have made a bad bargain.
It is the work which is honestly and thoroughly done
that does good all round. It does good to your master,
it does good to you ; it does good to the whole trade ;
it does good to your country ; in its measure it increases
the stock of wealth of the whole human race. Think
not that anything is lost which you put into your work
in the way of earnestness, truthfulness, energy and thor-
oughness. What you put into it you will get out of it,
only many times multiplied for your own and others'
blessing.

Some apprentices, and I fear their friends, and parents,
too, occasionally, are in a tremendous hurry to get at
results, at what they call " Tachlis." Five or six years
is a long time ; they are not earning much meanwhile,
and they say, " What is the good of it ? I might be
making a nice little sum every week, if I tried my hand
at something else." Don't be in a hurry to get at
results—all great results are got slowly—and even riches
made in a hurry are often like Jonah's gourd, which,
you know, grew up in a night and perished in a night.
Remember Moses and the eighty years that passed
before he entered upon his highest work. Be content
to wait and to let your work ripen—your reward also
will ripen in due time—of that you may be sure.

I remember when I and my brothers were children,
we lived in a house where there was a little garden, and
a few square feet of the garden were assigned to each
of us to cultivate for our amusement. We got some
seeds of fruit and flowers, and planted them. But like
other children we were very impatient, and we used to

go very stealthily to our plots of ground, and when we found that the plants were a long time coming, we would dig up the soil to see how they were getting on. There was the seed, it had already begun to germinate, the root was striking downwards, the stem was rising —but the plant never came to anything ; we had killed it, because we wanted to hurry it. Well, that did not perhaps matter much ; at the worst it meant the loss of a few pence; and the whole affair was, after all, a mere plaything. But, my lads, your work, your calling, your time, your life—these are no playthings ; and if you restlessly uproot what you, together with those who care for you and long to serve you, have already planted, the chance may never be yours again, and the loss may be irreparable.

Especially let me impress on you the duty of patiently and steadfastly continuing at that work to which, after proper consideration, you have bound yourselves. It is true we sometimes make a mistake in the vocation we have chosen, for all human brings are liable to error. But there is a worse and a more common mistake. It is the mistake of leaving one occupation for another, of quitting one trade and taking on another, and after being "everything by starts and nothing long," ending by knowing nothing and doing nothing worth speaking of for the rest of their days. These are the people who make a mess of their lives, and then blame the world for not recognizing how clever they were.

Depend upon it the very thing which many young fellows often regard as a hardship, the binding them-selves to five years' apprenticeship, more or less, is the salvation of them. If, in addition to a fair knowledge of a trade or handicraft they carry away with them habits of regularity, obedience and discipline, their time will have been indeed well spent, and their recompense greater than they themselves ever dreamed of.

And there is another and an immense advantage from the apprenticeship to which you are put under the direction of the Board of Guardians. It helps to foster in you a spirit of honourable independence. For it is no charity that is offered you, nor, I am sure, would you care, if you respect yourselves, to accept charity were it offered to you. Every time you repay the Board some of the expense incurred for your premium or your tools, you are not simply doing an act of common honesty, you are paying a tribute to your own manliness. I confess I envy (if envy is ever pardonable), I positively envy, the feelings of a young man at the moment when, as I know has often been the case, and as will be the case again with you, the last instalment of your debt has been paid, paid out of your own earnings, and a load is taken off your minds, and you go forth free from debt, not with less of gratitude but with more of self-respect, with the sense of self-reliance which stamps the true man ; when you can say, Now let others enjoy the benefit of what I have no right to any longer, and you thus show yourselves genuine descendants of your father Abraham, whose motto was, " I will not take from a thread to a shoe-latchet of all that is thine." It is by acts like these that you are helping to build up your own manhood, and the manhood of your people, and are adding strength and dignity to the glorious empire among whose sons you have shown yourselves fit and worthy to rank.

I wish it were possible to say that not a single one of our apprentices had ever done aught to cast dishonour on himself or the rest. I know that as a whole you have well maintained the credit of the Jewish name for honesty and truthfulness, but even one in a hundred convicted of lying or pilfering, or of any other offence, is enough to cast discredit on the rest, and I appeal to every one of you to maintain and even intensify, a feeling of brotherhood, of mutual responsibility among you, and to resolve, quite apart from any question of being found out and punished, never to do aught that shall degrade you or others, but so to fulfil your daily task that at its close you may be able to say, " Judge me, O Lord, according to my righteousness, and according to the integrity that is in me."

Now one great means of protecting you against temptation is provided by the very object with which you enter your master's shop, viz. work. " An idle mind is the devil's workshop." Work is the foe of all evil : of evil thoughts, of evil speech, of evil deeds, of evil companions, of all sins, big and little. Work is, in truth, a guardian angel. Some say that work is God's curse. Well, if work is God's curse, what must His blessing be ! But is it a curse ? It is related in the Midrash that when God pronounced the doom of Adam and said, " Thorns and thistles shall the earth bring forth for thee," tears burst from him, and he exclaimed, " Then there will be no difference between me and the beast ; I and the ass shall feed at one crib." But when God added, " In the sweat of thy brow thou shalt eat bread," Adam no longer grieved, but was well content with his fate. Even though Paradise be lost, no man can ever sink to the level of the brute who seeks in work a remedy for his sins and his sorrows, and knows that he is placed on earth not merely to consume his food, but to earn it.

So work is itself a protection against temptation and sin.

And another protection there is to which you should have recourse every day of your lives. When boys grow into young men they often give up a habit to which they were accustomed as children—the habit of prayer. They get to think it a waste of time. They go out to their work and make all sorts of acquaintances, and they get hold of some such catch word as that " to labour is better than to pray," as if the one were in the way of the other, or as if one would not rather work better after praying well.

I have read somewhere of a hero in Scottish history who, when he was being pursued by an overwhelming force, coolly dismounted from his horse to repair a flaw in the animal's harness. Those who watched him thought the man a fool ; he was wasting time. But meanwhile the flaw was mended, the clasp was fastened, the steed was mounted and the man had vanished. That broken buckle would have left him on the field, dead or a prisoner ; the timely delay of a few moments saved his life. So the youth who will not give a few moments to prayer before the day begins may find that he runs a terrible risk from dangers and temptations he never can altogether avoid ; he is badly equipped, and at any moment may be thrown and left inglorious in the dust.

But let him commence the day if only with a few minutes earnest communion with God ; let him for the time turn his back on the whole world, and concentrate his whole mind as he prays his ' Hear, O Israel," and " Thou shalt love the Lord thy God with all thy heart and soul and might " ; or offer up a fervent prayer, like that which is in our own Prayer Book. " Help us, O Lord our God, to understand Thy will and to do Thy commands ; let us not fall into the power of sin, transgression or temptation ; let not the evil inclination have power over us ; keep us far from bad men and bad companions ; make us cleave to the good inclination and to good works "—let him pray thus, and put his heart and soul into the words he utters, and he will discover that the time has not been wasted, but that he has gained immeasurably in vigour and decision of character and has been saved from the worst foes to a young man's peace and happiness of mind—while, as to his work, that will assuredly be all the more thorough and the more successful because of the spirit in which he will have set about it.

On the day when we shall be called to give an account of our life's work, the question that will be put to us all will be, not, hast thou had great opportunities ? not, hast thou done brilliant things ? but, hast thou done with thy might whatever thy hand found to do ? So may every one of you be able to answer that question, that, after having been diligent, patient and honest in your life's work, you too may be deemed worthy to stand before the King of kings, and to receive His blessing.

CHILDREN'S ORPHAN AID SOCIETY

(*New West End Synagogue, St. Petersburgh Place, W.,*
Feast of Tabernacles, October 2nd, 1893.)

PROVERBS XX. II : " Even a child is known by his doings,
whether his work be pure and whether it be right."

MY DEAR BOYS AND GIRLS,—In a certain part of Switzer-
land there is a mountain ridge, on which stands an inn.
To that inn a stable is attached. The stable has a roof,
a sloping roof, rising from the sides of the building, and
meeting in a line midway over the stable. Suppose a
drop of rain falls on that roof. One would fancy that
it could not make any difference whether it falls on one
side or on the other of the line. But what is the real fact ?
Why, this : If the drop of rain falls on one side of the
line or ridge of the roof, it will pass through a water-
spout into a little runnel, thence into a little brook,
which leads to a little river, which leads to a larger river,
which flows into a great stream, which falls into the
Mediterranean. But if the drop of rain falls on the
other side, at ever so small a distance off, then by similar
stages and channels it will after a while find its way into
the Atlantic Ocean. That is, a quarter of an inch
difference to-day, and in a few weeks these two drops
will be a thousand miles apart.

Now, boys and girls are very much like those drops
of rain. A very slight difference to their circumstances,

a trifling event in their lives, sometimes a single act of theirs, not much thought of at the time, may be sufficient to cause them to drift asunder, perhaps never to meet again.   I have known children of the same family, whom you would expect to find running side by side in the same channel all their lives, separated from one another by quite a trivial cause, and growing more strange to one another than if they had been perfect strangers.   And separated and estranged they were not only in their outward course of life, but, what is far more important, in their very hearts and characters. Some little difficulty conquered or not conquered, some little temptation resisted or not resisted, some childish habit checked or not checked in early life, has made the whole difference between a man or woman who now leads a useful, faithful, honourable, godly life, and one who lives to become a mere loafer, cumbering the earth, perhaps to be a disgrace and a grief to parents and kindred, and to defy the laws of God and man.   So you see that " even a child can be known by his doings, whether his work be pure and whether it be right."

But while there is a likeness between these drops of rain falling on this side or on that, and boys and girls turning to the right hand or to the left, you must remember that there is also a great unlikeness.   A drop of rain is a lifeless thing ; it merely follows the law of its nature when it falls where it falls, or is driven by a gust of wind hither and thither.   But you, boys and girls, have a mind, a conscience and a will—some of you rather a strong will, too—and you can settle for yourselves to a great extent whether you are going to join the right side or the wrong.   That you shall settle this for yourselves is the law of *your* nature.   A child *can* be known by his doings, whether his work be pure and whether it be right.

Now I want to tell you something which I hope won't make you vain. I don't know whether you have ever heard it before ; but if not, take my word for it. There is a great deal of good in every one of you. The question only is how to get it out of you, so that it may be of service to yourselves and others. You are all of you like so many blocks of marble. Inside every block of marble there is a beautiful statue. What does a sculptor do when he wants to carve a figure out of stone ? He takes his big block, and he cuts a bit away here and chips a bit away there, not too much, not too little, but just enough, and when he has got rid of all he doesn't want, and filed and smoothed away all the rough little bits and the sharp little bits—there is the statue. So is it with you. There is a lovely character hidden away in each of you—it only wants drawing forth. Education helps to draw it forth. Parents and teachers have to do much of the rough hewing and chipping away—which indeed in your unwisdom you sometimes complain of as being " rather rough on " you, though, by and by, when you are older and wiser, you will rejoice at the result. But the chief part of the task must be *yours* ; *you* must work at removing all that is evil, at bringing out and polishing and perfecting all that is good in you. Never has there been a truly good man who has not done the greater part of this work, requiring infinite patience and perseverance, for himself, and done it while he was yet young ; because it is the doings of the child that decide whether his whole life-work will be pure and right.

Therefore, dear children, my advice to you is this : Accustom yourselves early to chip away from your own characters bits of selfishness, greed, indolence, ill temper, cruelty, cowardice, meanness, and whatever else hides the good which I am sure is in you. Also accustom yourselves early to use in the best possible way all the gifts and opportunities with which God has blessed you. Do not say, " What can I do ? I am but a child ! "— " Small service is true service while it lasts," says the poet. God holds us responsible for every gift, or, to speak more correctly, for every loan of His. For in truth God never gives us anything out and out ; He only lends us what we think is ours ; He leaves it with us on trust, to be restored to Him. He trusts us with health, with youth, with talents, with money ; He trusts us with life, and one day He will assuredly ask of us an account of the way in which we have used these and all other loans and trusts.

I have read an Eastern story of a man who was going on a long journey. Before his departure, he put a couple of sacks of corn in charge of two of his acquaintances, giving one into the care of each. In due time, the traveller came back : " Where is my corn ? " he said to one. " All safe ! I tied up the mouth of the sack, and put it in the cellar. Take it again." So the sack was brought up and opened. And behold ! it was all mouldy and mildewed and utterly worthless. He went to the second. " Where is my corn ? " " Come out with me, and I will show it you." He took the man into a field all waving with golden wheat. "*There* is your corn." Then said the owner to the first man : " Take your reward—the sack of mildewed wheat you gave me." And to the second he said : " Give me back one sack of corn when the grain is threshed out—all the rest is yours."—When the time comes for God to claim back all the things He has placed in our charge, some there will be who will have nothing but rottenness to show, and they will receive their reward. What they give, that they will get. But some will have better husbanded and employed their trust, and they will reap as they have sown, only in much greater abundance. Theirs will be that " blessing of the Lord which maketh rich and addeth no sorrow thereunto."

But now to something personal and practical. I shouldn't be surprised if some of you were to say to me, " Sir, after what you have told us about there being such a quantity of good in us, we are really beginning to feel quite ' good ' in ourselves." That would be a pity. *Feeling* good is quite a different thing from *doing* good ; and if you mistake one for the other, you are only cheating yourselves. I would a hundred times sooner have a man feel bad and do good, than feel good and do nothing. Let me, then, point out to you how you can do some solid good, young as you are, and by your doings, even in the days of your childhood, give those who love you reason to hope that the sum and substance of your life's work will be pure and right.

I wonder if, when you are enjoying all the good and pleasant things with which the love of mother and father provides you, I wonder if you ever think of those who are without a father or without a mother, or, perchance, have neither father nor mother on this earth to work for them, to think and care for them, to lovingly correct them when they go astray, and lovingly encourage them when they strive to walk in the right path. Yet of such there are very, very many. And many more there are just as unfortunate—those who still have parents, but illness or accident, or other terrible misfortune has befallen them, and instead of being of help to their children and being able to support them, they themselves need help and support. I wish, dear children, you would compare your state with theirs. Think of your comfortable homes ; of the way you are watched over when you sleep and when you wake ; how you are guarded from danger and all evil, from cold and heat, and hunger and thirst ; how when you were ill, every one in the house was full of trouble on your account, and no end of pains were taken to make you well again, and how, when you were getting well, all sorts of loving-kindnesses were showered upon you in the way of delicacies, and books, and playthings, and amusements suited to your age and condition. All these things are yours because you have parents who love you, and who do not leave off loving you, though you are at times fractious, and obstinate, and even unthankful. And all these things are lacking to hundreds and thousands of other children, most of them not a bit worse than you, and many of them a good deal better. It is not *their* fault that they are without father and mother ; it is not *your* merit that you are doubly rich through having both. Would it not be a good thing if you, who enjoy what they so sadly miss, were to come to their aid ? They are children like you ; unlike you only in misfortune.

How to do it ? The easiest thing in the world. Are there any of you who can spare out of your pocket-money or from presents you sometimes get, or from any other source, *one penny* a week ? I think I ought rather to put the question in another way ! Are there any among you who *can't* spare a penny a week for some unselfish purpose ? When I think of the amount of money that children waste, even children who haven't got rich parents, I have no difficulty in answering this question. Well, make up your minds to-day to deprive yourselves of something to the extent of one penny every week in order that poor fatherless and motherless children may have a little of that happiness of which you have so much. Promise to-day that you will regularly put that sum in a money box, or give it in charge of your parents, for the support of orphans, and others equally unfortunate who are received into our great Orphan Asylum. And try to get other boys and girls to promise the same.

Why do I ask you to make this resolution to-day ? Because to-day is a holy day, of which the Bible says, " Thou shalt rejoice on thy festival." And then it goes on to say, " Not only thou, but thy son and thy daughter and thy manservant and thy maidservant, and the stranger, the Levite, and the *orphan* and the widow, who are in thy gates." You see our Heavenly Father tells us that there can be no true joy, if we keep it all to ourselves. True joy overflows the heart and pours itself upon others, upon those dear to us, first, and then upon those who, though more distant, are not less in need of rejoicing than our own. God, it is true, is the Father of the fatherless ; but let us not forget that we are their brothers and sisters. There are many people who seem to fancy that festival is a word of one syllable, and spells *f, e, a, s, t.* It would be better to understands " festival " to mean *festive all*—a day when *all* should be festive.

And what is it you will be giving up if you do what you are now entreated to do ? Perhaps a pennyworth of sweets or of other pleasure every week. But what is so sweet a pleasure as to feel that you have, in your way and according to your means, helped to house and feed and clothe and educate some poor, forsaken, father-less and motherless child, perhaps have even had a share in saving the life of some orphaned boy or girl ?   I have heard of a boy who was an expert swimmer, and who once rescued a person from drowning.   And the sensa-tion was so delightful to him that afterwards he was always longing that, wherever he went, people might be drowning, so that he might have the joy and delight of saving them !   That, however, is a treat which, you will understand, cannot be afforded you every week. But here is one constantly ready to hand for every one of you—the happiness of helping to preserve and bless some forlorn young life.   "Happy," says the Psalmist, "is he who doeth charity continually."   " Who is it," ask our ancient sages, " that does charity con-tinually ?   It is he who takes an orphan child under his care ;   for he is doing one long act of charity during all the years the child is being reared and trained for the duties of life."

Will you not, dear children, take your part in such a work of love ?   You could not possibly make a better beginning in real good doing.   True, what you can give may be only a drop in the ocean ;   but the ocean is made up of mere drops.   Now, on the one side of you is the vast ocean of self-indulgence and extravagance, full to overflowing, into which so many people, young as well as old, are ever pouring nearly all they possess ;   on the other side is the sea of charity, from which more and more has to be drawn and which sometimes threatens to run dry.   On which side shall your drop fall ?   God help you in this and in all things to make a right and pure choice.

AFTER THE HOLIDAYS

(*Delivered at the Thanksgiving Service in connexion with the Poor Children's Country Holiday Fund, at the Great Synagogue, Sabbath, October 27th, 1894.*)

GENESIS ii. 8 : " And the Lord God planted a garden in Eden."

I WANT to welcome you all very heartily, dear boys and girls, who have come here this afternoon to offer thanks to God for the pleasant holiday you have had. I take it for granted that you have all enjoyed yourselves very much, not with a make-believe, but with a real enjoyment, so much, in fact, that, when next summer comes round, if you should get such another chance, there will not be the least objection on your part to repeat your trip to the country or to the sea-side. And I also take it for granted that your stay out of town has not only been agreeable to you, but especially agreeable to others, to the cottagers and superintendents and other friends who had charge of you ; that you left a good character behind you, and that all those who had anything to do with you were so charmed with your behaviour that they are burning to see you again, and to do the same service for you next year as they did this. If I am mistaken in any of you or if I am taking too much for granted, you can tell me about it after service, when we shall be able to have a little private conversation together.

37

There is one thing about which I am sure I am not mistaken, and that is, that all of you who have been to the country cannot help loving the country. That is a good and hopeful sign. That is a sign that you have an unspoilt heart, for the pleasures of the country are innocent pleasures, and those who never tire of them will never quite lose their innocence. Who was it planted the first garden ? " God first planted a garden." And whom did He put into it ? Adam and Eve. Why ? Because a garden was the very place for good and simple-hearted people to be happy in. God wished them to be happy, and accordingly into the Garden of Eden He put them, which, as many of you who have learnt Hebrew know, means the Garden of Pleasure, the Garden of Happiness.

However, your holiday is over now. Country and gardens, you have left them behind you. You are back again in London town, and back for work. What have you brought with you out of your holiday ? What have you brought from the country into the town and into this synagogue ?

First and foremost, I hope you have brought with you a feeling of thankfulness to God Almighty that He has made His world such a beautiful world, beautiful with a loveliness, ever fresh and varying, in hills and valleys and plains, in trees and grass and flowers, in rivers, and seas, and in the great and glorious expanse of heaven that stretches above our heads, but that can never be properly seen until we get outside our streets of bricks and mortar, and well into the country. Thankfulness to God is then your first duty, and that not only because He has made the world so beautiful, but because you yourselves have been able to see and enjoy so much of its beauty, so that you may well repeat the Psalmist's words : " Bless the Lord, O my soul : O Lord, my God, Thou art very great ; Thou hast robed Thee in grandeur and majesty ; Thou coverest Thyself with light as with a garment ; Thou stretchest out the heavens like a curtain."

Next, you ought to have come back with a feeling of gratitude to those human friends whose kindness has helped you to spend a time among these lovely objects of God's world. But for them I doubt very much whether one in twenty or in fifty among you would this year have caught a glimpse of the green fields and glistening sea, and, if you had, whether you would not have lacked something that is very necessary indeed for the proper enjoyment of a stay in the country. Have you ever noticed the curious effect which a great deal of fresh air and bodily exercise have upon the digestion ? Well, your friends noticed it, and they provided accordingly. I learn on all sides that the appetites both of the girls and boys who were sent out by the Committee of the Children's Country Holiday Fund were all, and more than all, that could be desired. Did you ever hear the story of the trusting boy and the wicked fairy ? A boy once found a cup belonging to a fairy. To induce him to give it up to her, she promised to give him the strength of twelve men. You will readily understand that the boy was delighted with the bargain, and as he returned the cup to the fairy, he found that he really did obtain the strength of twelve men. But then a strange and a terrible thing happened. With the strength of twelve men, he got also the appetite of twelve men, but, as the cunning fairy had said nothing about food, he had, notwithstanding the appetite of twelve men, to content himself with the food of one boy only. What that boy suffered I must leave to your imagination to picture. Well, that has just been the way your friends have *not* acted towards you. They have been good fairies, and if they did you one favour, the effect of which was to increase your hunger, they did not omit the other, by which they strove to satisfy the improved appetite they had themselves produced. I say, then, that you have reason to be doubly thankful to them for this two-fold kindness.

What else have you brought away with you ? A stock of good health, I trust—one of God's greatest blessings. Without it, though you were a great and mighty monarch, lord over a hundred provinces, ruler over millions of people, with a dozen castles and palaces of your own, you might still be one of the most pitiable of beings. With it, whatever else you may lack, life will have countless joys for you. You have brought with you from the country a store of health and strength which, I hope, you have not used up, and which will last you for months to come. And in this you are not the only ones who have benefited. Your fathers and mothers in many cases have been less fortunate than you : for them there has been no country holiday ; but they have been happy in knowing you to be well, and from many a father's and mother's heart the prayer has arisen : Thank God for the mercy done to us in making our children well and strong.

Then, again, you ought to have carried away with you the joys of memory. I will tell you what I mean. Memory is that gift of God by which we can multiply as many times as we like, wherever and whenever we like, whatever we have once experienced. In the dark and dreary days of winter, you have merely to say to yourself, Now, what was I doing in the country six months ago ?—and instantly it will all start to your minds again, and you will see once more the lovely sights, and hear the pleasant sounds, and smell the sweet odours of the country, and you might even shut your eyes and fancy yourself lying in the grass again, with the birds singing about you, while you seem to yourself gazing at the skies above, with their white and blue and fleecy clouds sailing past ; and all God's world will grow once more so exceeding beautiful. You have been companions with one another during your holiday ; talk it all over again with one another. We who love you wish that your childhood especially should be a bright and happy period for you, for to be happy then is to have a source of happiness in joyous recollections all your lives. Such magic is there in memory.

If you want something to keep your remembrance of the country fresh, let me suggest this to you. I wonder how many of you keep and cultivate flowers in your homes ? Now, boys and girls who have seen something of flowers in the country, ought to take care that some of these lovely creations of God should always have a place in their windows or in some other convenient spot in their homes. It costs very little. An old box can be used in place of a flower pot, and a few pence, such as even very poor children manage to get and spend not always very wisely, would suffice to buy a little mould and a few flower seeds ; and a wonderful change would come over whole rows of dull, dismal-looking houses, for there would soon be no house without its pretty window-garden.

And lastly, dear children, I hope you have not returned

from your pleasant trip without a store of unselfish thoughtfulness for those who were less lucky than you. I know that a good many of you have already given proofs of such thought and loving regard for others. I refer to those among you who brought back some small memorial of their visit, such as plants or flowers, for their dear ones who had to stay at home, so that they too might have some share in your enjoyment. It is a curious thing that enjoyment makes bad people worse, but makes good people better. Talking of unselfishness, I have heard such a touching story in connexion with the Children's Country Holiday that I can't resist telling it to you. There were two children—members of a very poor family—one was a girl of twelve, the other a boy of about ten. They were both put on the list of children to be sent into the country by the local Committee, but the parents were too poor to pay their part of the expenses for more than one. Now, the girl had been to the country last year, but she had been dangerously ill in the spring, and, though she had recovered, was still extremely weak. The boy had never yet been out on a country holiday. Then there arose a great dispute between this brother and this sister—and what do you think about ? —it was not because each wanted to go, but because each wanted the other to go. " You," said Jane to George (those were not their real names, but I call them so because, for their sakes, I don't want you to know them), " you," said Jane, with the air of a loving elder sister, " you must go ; first, you are younger, and, besides, you have never been." " Not I," said George, who had ideas of his duty as a male, "you have been ill, and I heard the doctor say that you will never get all your strength back unless you get some country air ;

you must go, and come back well and strong, and I shall be quite happy to know that you are happy." There was no settling this dispute between a brother and sister, neither of whom would be outdone by the other in tenderness and self-sacrifice, and the result would have been that neither the one nor the other would have gone, had it not been that, at the last moment a kind-hearted lady, hearing of the case, came to the rescue and paid the amount needed for the home contribution for one of the children. It is the unselfish example of that brother and sister that you, dear children, should strive to imitate, and more pleasure and higher happiness will be yours than you ever dreamt of.

Certainly, you must not imagine that because you have left the country behind you, all your pleasures are at an end. Heaven forbid! Just think of the words with which I began: "And the Lord God planted a garden *in* Eden." You see, then, that *Eden* was larger than the *garden*; and it may also well be that many of you, though you have no garden any more, may still be moving about in Eden, that is, in happiness. A great many people have tried to find out where Eden was, and have travelled far in search of it. One learned German has written a whole work on "Where was Paradise?" and I can show you a table drawn up by another learned man giving thirty-two different places, each of which was believed to be the very place where to look for Eden. The fact of the matter is, there are plenty of people who remind one of the old gentleman who went rummaging about the house intently looking for something. "What are you looking for?" said his little granddaughter. "For my spectacles," replied the grandfather. "Why, they are on your nose," said the little girl. So are there people who fancy that happiness is always to be found at a distance and in out-of-the-way places when, if they only had the sense to know it, they could discover it quite close to them, and wherever they went. " The eyes of a *fool* are in the ends of the earth," said the wise man. If you go the right way about it, you will not fail to find happiness for yourselves in town as well as in country. And this is what the Bible says : " If thou wilt hearken unto the voice of the Lord thy God to observe and do all His commandments, blessed shalt thou be in the city, and blessed shalt thou be in the field."

Yes, dear boys and girls, happiness will be yours not merely while you are holiday-making, but while you are labouring so as to fit yourselves for, and in some measure to deserve, a holiday. Not even the Garden of Eden was a place of idleness. God put man into it " to till it and to guard it." There is an Arabian story that, when God had made the Garden of Eden, He commanded the Garden to speak its thoughts. The Garden pondered a little and then said : " There is no God but God." But though this was a great truth, God was not satisfied with the answer, and so he ordered the Garden to speak once more. Then the Garden pondered again and in a little while said : " The faithful shall be happy." Again God said that this was a great truth, but that He was not satisfied with the answer, and so he ordered the Garden to speak for the third time. Then the Garden pondered long and after a considerable interval said : " Those who are idle and think only of pleasure shall never enter me." And God said that this answer was good.

And so it will be with you. Work, and not an endless

holiday and idle lounging even in the loveliest places on earth, work it is that will make of you boys and girls true men and women, true Jews and Jewesses ; hard honest work for the present at school and by and by outside it in whatever station of life God may call you to ; work, not for yourselves alone, but for others as well, for your nearest and dearest and perhaps, Heaven helping you, for all your fellow-men. And then, if you go about your duties blessed with health and strength, thankful to your Friend in Heaven and to your earthly friends, delighting in happy memories, striving to lead pure and unselfish lives, you will find that your Eden is everywhere, and that in your heart of hearts God Himself has planted the *Garden* of Eden.

QUEEN VICTORIA

(At the Children's Memorial Service, Great Synagogue, 1901.)

I KINGS iii. : " In Gibeon the Lord appeared to Solomon in a dream by night : and God said, Ask what I shall give thee. And Solomon said . . . give Thy servant an understanding heart to judge Thy people, that I may discern between good and evil. . . . And God said unto him, Because thou hast asked this thing . . . behold, I have done according to thy word. . . . And I have also given thee that which thou hast not asked. . . . And Solomon awoke ; and, behold, it was a dream."

IT is a wonderful story. The young King has been left alone. His father, David, had gone the way of all living, and the boy ruler, who, at the time was about fifteen years of age, was called to fill a place of great honour, of great responsibility and of great danger. He began his task by seeking the favour of God, by whom kings and queens do reign. That same night, after he had offered sacrifices to God, according to the custom of the time, the Lord appeared unto him, and made him that offer, which many a youth and maiden has dreamt of before and since : " Ask what I shall give thee ! " And Solomon remembering what his father, David, before him had been in the sight of God and thinking of what was now expected of himself, answered " Give me wisdom." He showed his wisdom by asking for wisdom— wisdom for what purpose ? Wisdom to know and to do the sacred duties of his high office, to discern between good and evil, to be a true and just ruler over a great people. And God replied to him, as you have just heard, promising him what he had asked for, and more— all the other things on which people usually set their hearts, but which he had not asked for. " And Solomon awoke ; and, behold, it was a dream." *Was* it all a dream ? It began as a dream, it ended as a reality.

Nearly sixty-four years ago, very early one summer's morning, there was a great knocking and ringing at Kensington Palace, where was lying, fast asleep, the Princess Victoria. Two great officers of State, the Archbishop of Canterbury and the Lord Chamberlain, had hurried thither to awaken her, and to tell her that, William IV being dead, she was Queen. It took some time to arouse the household. The visitors desired an audience of Her Royal Highness. The attendant pleaded that the Princess was in such a sweet sleep she would not venture to disturb her. " We are here on business of State to the *Queen*, and even her sleep must give way to that." Then after a little while the Princess hurried into the room, her eyes dim with tears, scarcely knowing whether she was awake or asleep. Was it a dream ? she might have said to herself. But when she realized what it all meant, and was informed of her new dignity, her first words were : " I ask your prayers on my behalf." And they knelt down together, and Victoria began her reign like the young King of Israel, by asking from the King of kings, the most High God, an understanding heart to judge so great a people.

Yesterday they bore her to her grave after a life rich not only in years and might and glory and renown, but in the very highest wisdom—in the wisdom of love. And if you were to inquire of any one who has studied

her career, What about the promise of her youth ?
he would have to answer, The promise of her youth ?
She spent every day of the sixty-three years of her reign
in fulfilling it.   No wonder that to-day the memory of
that good, true, faithful, loving, lovable woman is blessed
by all her people.

Many years after she had come to the throne her
old governess wrote her a letter, in which she reminded
the Queen of what had occurred when first she became
aware that she was most likely to succeed to the Crown
of the United Kingdom.   The Princess Victoria was at
the time twelve years old, and not until then did she have
an inkling of what was in store for her.   Then it was that,
with the consent of her mother, her tutor put into her
history book a table of genealogies, and when she opened
it, and read it, she said, " I never saw that before.   I see
I am nearer to the throne than I thought," and then, as
the meaning of it all became clearer to her, she thought
of the burden as well as of the honour that would be
hers, and feeling that she had not always been as serious
as she might have been in her studies and other things,
she seized her teacher's hand, exclaiming again and
again, " I will be good, I will be good."

That was, indeed, the noblest resolution with which
to begin a royal life.   It meant, I want to do my duty
in the place to which God has called me.   Not, I will be
great, I will be rich, I will be feared, but, I will be good.
It is exactly the same as that for which Solomon prayed
when he said, " Give Thy servant an understanding
heart to judge Thy people, that I may discern between
good and evil."

Many a child, even many a clever child, has made
a failure of his life because he thought that the only

things worth striving for were riches and power, and glory and victory, and forgot that, unless he put goodness first, all the other gifts are curses and not blessings, both to others and to himself. No such fatal mistake was made by Queen Victoria. And it almost seems as if the old story had repeated itself in her case, word for word, as if God had said to her, Behold, I have done according to thy word, I have given thee a wise and understanding heart—and I have also given thee that which thou hast not asked.

Very beautiful it is, and to you I hope especially interesting, to think of her as she was in her childhood and youth. It was not a childhood without trials, for she lost her father before she was a year old, and so missed the treasure not only of a father's love for his child, but of a child's love for a father. But she was fortunate in having a mother who did her utmost to fill up that great gap in her life, and devoted all her thought and labour to train her child worthily for the high place she was destined to fill.

The effect of such training showed itself early in the Princess' character. Thus we learn how strictly truthful she was as a little child. Her teacher, Dr. Davys, many years after told the following anecdote about her young days. One day during lessons she had become very restless and impatient for the work to be over. Her mother, the Duchess of Kent, came in and asked how she had behaved. " Oh," said the governess, who had been in the room during the time, " once she was rather troublesome." " No," said the Princess, touching her governess, " twice—don't you remember ? "

One marked virtue in our beloved Queen was that she was always faithful to her friends. To have served

her once was to be ever remembered by her. Of course
as people grow older, they are likely to lose by death
those whom they knew and loved in earlier years, and it
was the fate of our dear Queen, whom God blessed with
a life of more than eighty years, to outlive most of her
early friends and companions. But while they lived she
never forgot them, whether they were relations, playmates,
servants, nurses, or teachers ; for them all she had a place
in her heart, especially for those who taught her, and when
they fell ill she would visit and try to console and cheer
them, and when God called them from this world she
would honour their memory in a way that was as much
an honour to her as to them. That, dear children, is one
of the marks by which you may know a noble soul from
a vulgar one. A vulgar soul gets tired of old friends, likes
to get rid of them, tries to forget them, and is always
looking out for new and what is thought better acquaintances. A true and noble soul clings to old friends,
because, when he has no need of them, he still has need
of their love, and knows he does not deserve their love
unless he continues to give them his. " Thine own
friend and thy father's friend forsake not," says the
Holy Book. The Queen was ever mindful of that lesson.

Another great quality of hers was her watchful-
ness. Nothing that it behoved her to know and to do
escaped her. And there is no doubt that one reason
why the people of England have so long felt so safe, why
they could take their rest without fear, was that they
had a Queen who was on the watch, and that as was the
Sovereign so would her ministers and servants have to
be, watchful exceedingly over the safety, the interests,
the welfare of her people.

For instance, from the beginning of her reign already,

it is said the Queen insisted that when any of those accidents occurred that send a shock of horror through the public mind, the most searching inquiry should be made. She was determined to have it known how the misfortune happened, why it happened, and whether it could not be prevented for the future. When the Queen felt warmly on a subject, she was in the habit of expressing herself warmly ; and careless, easy-going people, on whom the lives of others depended, had to mend their ways, while parliament, fired by the zeal of the Queen, as well as by the needs of the people, made better and better laws for their safety and protection.

Yes, she was watchful over all and untiringly wakeful. Those who are apt to think what a pleasant, easy time a queen must have, have no idea of the constant and tremendous strain there was upon Her Majesty. Every day brought its work, and plenty of it, work of the utmost consequence that could not be put off till the morrow. When the rest of the Court had retired for the night, the Queen would be at work still, often far into the morning. A curious illustration of this is given in what is told concerning one of the Queen's menservants, who had to be dismissed because he had fallen asleep and neglected his duty, which was to put out the lamps in the private apartments of the Queen. " How can a man be expected to keep awake half the night ? " he murmured. But what the servant could not do, his royal mistress did— and often when the world outside was wrapped in sleep, she was working, watching, planning, toiling for the good of her people.

Another most lovable quality of hers was her intense love for children—her own children, her grandchildren, her great-grandchildren, the children of her servants, of

the peasants she met on her outings, the children of the
schools that have grown and increased so wonderfully
during her reign. Some of you here or some of your
brothers and sisters were, perhaps, present at the Queen's
review of school children during her Diamond Jubilee.
In all that happy time, which brought her innumerable
signs of dutiful homage and love from her people in every
part of the globe, there was nothing that gave her greater
pleasure than that assembly of 10,000 school children,
who had a little royal review and procession all to themselves on Constitution Hill. And very beautiful and
touching was her reply to all the good wishes that were
expressed to her on behalf of the children—that she
hoped for a great deal from the education they were now
receiving, and that those who were now children might
grow up in a State blessed with even greater happiness
and welfare than have already been vouchsafed to our
generation.

Yesterday there was another procession in London.
It bore with every mark of honour and of mourning
the body of our Queen to her last resting-place—by the
side of her beloved husband whose image was never out
of her heart, or, indeed, out of her sight.

But we must not part, dear children, this afternoon
with only sorrow in our hearts. Amidst all the sadness
with which our hearts have been filled, there are two
things to congratulate ourselves upon. First, we have
had the happiness to live in the reign of a Queen under
whose government more has been done for the good of
the people than in the lifetime of any other monarch who
has sat upon the throne, a reign during which we Jews
have come to be treated on a perfect equality with the
rest of the people of this country, and every real grievance

of which we have ever had to complain has been got rid of. That is something for you to remember, something for you to talk about hereafter to other children. You will be able to say to them. " I lived in the reign of Queen Victoria the Good."

And next we have reason to rejoice that we are now living under a Sovereign who has already shown himself a true son of his mother. That is proved by the first words he spoke to his first council immediately after his succession, when he declared that he would give himself, as long as life was his, to the well-being of his people and the welfare of his Empire. There have now been seven Edwards Kings of England. But we Jews have only known two—the first and the latest Edward. What a difference between our fate under the one and under the other ! In the time of Edward I all the Jews of England were either forced to be false to their religion, or were ruthlessly driven out of the land, ruined, helpless, almost hopeless, to seek in other countries a shelter they were nowhere allowed to enjoy for long. In the time of Edward VII we are living under a Sovereign who makes no distinction among his subjects, be their religion what it may, and under laws which make it possible for Jews and Jewesses to fill any position for which they are fit, and to serve, as they were never allowed before—to *serve* as well as to love their country. We should, indeed, be ungrateful—God forbid that we should ever deserve such a reproach !—if we did not value our blessings and prove that we value them by striving, all of us, old and young, rich and poor, to do our duty as loyal citizens of our country, and as faithful subjects of our King, whom may God bless and preserve long and happily to reign over us.

HIGH AIMS

*(New West End Synagogue,
8th day of Tabernacles, October 15th, 1900.)*

EXODUS xxiv. 12 : " And the Lord said unto Moses, Come up
to Me into the Mount, and be there."

HAVE you ever noticed how often mountains are mentioned in the Bible, and how fond the holy men of old
were of them ? You remember that Noah's Ark rested
on a mountain. When Abraham was going to prove
his love for and faith in God, he took his son Isaac,
whom he thought he was to offer to God, up to a mountain, Mount Moriah. When Jacob made a covenant
with Laban, each promising that he would be friends
with the other, it was on Mount Gilead that promise was
made. Jerusalem, the chief city in the Holy Land, was
built on a mountain, Mount Zion. Elijah taught the
false priests who the true God was on Mount Carmel,
and so on.

But there is no man in whose story mountains play
such a part as Moses. He feeds Jethro's flock by a
mountain, and he hears God's voice saying to him,
" When thou bringest forth My people from Egypt, you
shall serve God on this mountain." On that mountain
the Ten Commandments were given ; there it was that
Moses went up to receive the tables of stone, being there
forty days and nights ; and after he had broken the
tables in displeasure for his people's sin, to that moun-

tain he returned, staying there another period of forty days and nights. Later on he and his brother Aaron are told to go up Mount Hor, and on that mountain Aaron, the high priest, dies. And when his own time comes to leave this world, he, as the very last act of his life, ascends Mount Nebo, even to the top of Pisgah, from which he gets a view of the whole country his people were to possess, and there he dies, his body being buried on the mount, no one knows where, but his pure and saintly spirit, rising higher still, returning unto God who gave it.

Now there must be some reason why mountains were so often chosen for these great and sacred purposes. One reason probably is that mountains are grand and impressive objects. One can't help gazing at them with wonder and amazement. They look like great giants, and they do make us all, even the big people among us, look so small. Another reason, no doubt, is that on a mountain one somehow feels freer, one breathes a purer air, one gets a larger and a grander view. The common parts of the earth seem farther off, and we ourselves seem to be nearer heaven.

But I fancy there must be another reason still. To get up a mountain you must climb—at least you had to in former times ; now they sometimes make it easier, and you can get carried all the way by a special sort of train, but formerly no one could get to a great height without toil and labour, inch by inch, step by step, foot by foot, until the summit was reached.

And this is what the mountains of the Bible seem to say to us, especially the mountains in the history of Moses, about whose last ascent we shall read in the synagogue to-morrow : Have a high aim, ye children of men : do not be satisfied with the low, the mean things ; fix your mind on something higher, on the highest. And strive for it inch by inch, foot by foot ; be determined to climb your way. Do not be satisfied when you have gone a little way, and say to yourself, Well, that is all that can be expected of me. God asks every one of us to do his best, and it is only the best that each can do that satisfies Him.

Can you say to yourselves, dear children, I am doing my very best. I am doing my best at school. God has given me a certain amount of sense ; I am making the best use I can of that. I am doing my best at home to make others about me happy, and to give back a full measure of my love in return for all the love I receive. When I think of God's goodness round about me, and of God Himself above me, I try my utmost to please Him, to lift up my soul to Him. Can you say that to yourselves ?

It is true, dear children, it often happens that a person has very high and noble aims and does not succeed in them. I think we have all of us, even the smallest and the weakest among us, sometimes a desire to do something really great and really good, but somehow it doesn't come off. Well, that need not distress us over much. It does not follow that because we sometimes slip in trying to get up a mountain that we shall never get there at all. The hope and the desire and effort— these are the chief things, and these help us all a very long way up, even if we do not reach the very top.

A boy or girl with no ambition never does anything worth mentioning. If you care for nothing, you will do nothing ; but if you care for something really great and good, though you may not be able to accomplish it, you will do something at all events greater and better than if you cared for nothing at all.

There was once a youth who left his home for the first time to go out into the world and make his way for himself. After a while he came to a broad fast-flowing stream which he wanted to cross. He wanted to get to a village which lay exactly opposite to the spot which he had reached on one side of the river. So he hired a boat and told the boatman to row him right across. But the boatman, instead of rowing straight across, directed the vessel up the river and pulled with all his might up stream, as though he wanted to land high up above the village.

"Where are you going?" said the youth. "Straight across," answered the boatman. "If that is straight I have lost my power of seeing clear. At this rate we shall land four or five hundred yards above the village." "Yes," replied the boatman, "if we can keep on like this. But there is little chance of that. The force of the stream, when we have reached the middle, will drive us back far enough." And in point of fact the boatman in the end had to put forth all his strength not to be drawn far away and below his aim. As the youth was about to get out of the boat the man said to him, "You seem to be starting in life. Take an old man's advice. I had it from my old father. He used to say that a good lad starting in life is like a good river boatman. He should fix his aim somewhat too high, else he will be carried down too low. The one is carried down by the current of the stream, the other by what is called the current of the world, that is, by the strong temptations and the many evil examples he meets with in the world. Therefore aim high." The youth said good-bye and paid his fare. He also took that advice to heart. Many years after he came that same way and crossed with the same boatman, and remembering him he paid him a double fare ; for, he said, a man who gives me a good lesson as well as a safe crossing has done me a double service, and deserves double thanks.

Have a high aim—that is one part of the lesson I want you to take away with you—but never flatter yourself you have reached it, that is the other and not less important part.

I remember once being at the house of a lady whose daughter had just returned from the last school she was to attend. The mother was proud of her child, and said she had reason to be, because her daughter had completed her education at a first-rate finishing school. I saw and conversed with the young lady, and I am bound to say she did not strike me as being exactly finished. She rather appeared to me to have been just begun. If she *was* finished, she was certainly badly finished. No good school claims to be a finishing school. Do not imagine, dear boys and girls, that you will ever be finished in any school in the world. For that your whole life is needed, and every moment of it. And all the time your aims must grow and your minds and hearts be fixed on something higher and ever higher

It will be a bad day for you when you say, now I have enough knowledge ; it will be an even worse day if ever you should say, I am good enough. In certain parts of the world there is a kind of fly called a fire-fly. It has the curious quality that it can shine in the night like a bright spot. But it only shines while it is flying. The moment it folds its wings and rests, it is dark. So it is with our soul. So long as it is active in gaining wisdom

and in helping others to get it, in gathering goodness and
in making others good, it is the bright and beautiful, the
brightest and the most beautiful perhaps in all creation ;
but the instant it stops, it darkens and loses all its
beauty and its brightness.

And the same thing is taught us by all that long run
of holy days one after the other at this sacred season.
First, as you know, we have New Year. Well, that is a
great day—it is a sign of God's favour to us in giving
us another year of life, and it ought to make us very
happy. Then comes another holy day we have to observe, the Day of Atonement, and if that is well spent
we may be sure that we have God's forgiveness for
any evil we may have done and have truly repented of.
And that ought to make us happier still. But we have
not yet done ; on the top of that comes the Feast of
Tabernacles for a whole week, and that promises us that
God's kindness is going to be continued to us, and that
ought to make us feel happy. And then just as that
festival is coming to an end there comes another, a sort
of " good-bye and don't forget to come again " kind of
festival. That is to-day. But do not imagine it is all
over yet, for there is yet another festival to come to-
morrow—the festival of " Rejoicing in the Law," and
to know God's will and to do it. Why, to any boy or
girl, or for the matter of that to any man or woman, of a
right disposition, to know God's will, and to do it, there
is no greater happiness than that in all the world. And
how do we celebrate that—by stopping ? Not at all ;
by beginning all over again, for no sooner have we
finished reading God's Law than we commence it over
again, and so by these means we learn that there is no
standing still in the knowledge and the doing of good,

but it is always onward, onward, upward, upward, until God says to us, Come up to Me into the Mount and be (i.e., stay) there.

Do you know, dear children, there are some who have already answered to God's call ?

I wonder if you have noticed—those of you who are old enough surely must have done so—that there is a part of to-day's service in the synagogue which calls to our minds those who have gone away from us and have gone up to God. That part of the service is called " the prayer of remembrance for the souls " of those who have passed away from us. Happily most of you are blessed with good and loving parents who still are with you to love and guard you. But some, and especially the older ones among us, are not so fortunate, and the thought of those whom we have lost comes back or ought to come back to us very often, especially on the anniversary or date of their death, and on every festival of the year. It will make the day more holy to us if we think of our dear parents and other beloved ones, and remember that they have gone up the mount to God, and that however much they tried to come nearer to God while their bodies lived, they are nearer to Him now their bodies are dead. For as a wise and good man of old once said, " The souls of the righteous are in the hand of God, and no evil shall befall them " (Wisdom 3). And if that is so with men and women who have led good lives, though not perfect, it is not less so with little children who never did much harm to any one and whom God has taken up to Himself.

It is very right, I think, to call them to mind even in our joyful days, not to make us sad, but to make us grateful that we had them with us once, and to make us wish and strive to be like them, in their innocence, or in their courage to fight against evil and to work for good. While we are alive God says to us " Come up," elevate your characters, your lives, by being good and honest and pure. And when the day comes for God to say to you for the last time, " Come up to Me into the Mount, and be there," the higher and higher you have climbed in your young days the easier will it be to make the last ascent, the nearer you will already be to the top. So be glad to-day that God has asked you to get near to him, be happy in your strength to rise, and make your life, every hour of it, a step nearer and nearer to the Lord who loves you and raises you up.

"THE CHILD WAS A CHILD"

(*Borough Synagogue*, 1891.)

I SAMUEL i. 24: "And the child was a child."

I AM not going to tax your knowledge of Hebrew very much this morning, because the text—and every sermon must have a text—on which I want to speak to you consists of only two Hebrew words, and what is still more fortunate the first word is the same as the second. It is taken from the early history of the prophet Samuel. Many, nay, I would hope all of you, remember the beautiful story, how Hannah came with her husband year by year, most likely on this very festival, to worship and sacrifice unto the Lord in Shiloh ; how she grieved that God had not blessed her with a child, and how when her prayer had been fulfilled, she remembered the vow she had made in her sorrow, waited only until her boy was sufficiently old to be conscious of his own actions, and then took him with her to the priest Eli, saying as she presented him, " This is the child for which I have prayed. I lend him to the Lord all the days of his life." It is just before this last event that the words occur to which I want you to closely attend : " And the child was a child." The English Bible translates it, " and the child was young." But that is not quite exact and does not seem to give all the true meaning that lies in the literal translation : " The boy was a boy," or " the child was a child."

There are perhaps some here this morning who might feel inclined to say : Well, there is not much information in that. " The boy was a boy," or " the child was a child." Of course he was. He wasn't a man, or else he wouldn't have been a boy. To those who would jump at that ready answer, I can only say that is just the admission I wanted you to make. It seems to me also, though I take the words perhaps in a wider sense than you do, that a child is and should be a child, that a boy is not and should not be a man, and a girl is not and should not be a woman.

If you examine for yourselves the first three chapters of the First Book of Samuel, you will find that term the child, the boy Samuel, over and over again. Whoever wrote that sacred story, whether Samuel himself or some one else, appears to have been determined that no one should make a mistake about that matter. It is the *child-nature* of Samuel that is to be clearly brought before all the world as an example. He lived in stirring and anxious times, amid many and sore temptations ; yet, until the Providence of God ripened him into a man, he lived, and spoke, and acted, and thought, and prayed, as a child.

And this is the lesson which the child Samuel teaches you—a lesson that never deserved to be better weighed and heeded than now, in the very age in which you live : Be not as children anything but children ; do not attempt to be men and women before your time. Do not think it a fine thing or a clever thing to give yourselves the airs and pretensions of man- or womanhood while Heaven still blesses you with childhood. Nature condemns it ; your fellow-men dislike it ; God would not have it. Nature will not have it ; she has set her face against it, against your being men and women before your time. Have you ever had your attention drawn to this remarkable arrangement in Nature—that the higher you go in the scale of animals, the longer, you will find, it takes for any creature to reach maturity. A fly or a worm finds its own sustenance almost immediately after it begins to live. In a few days or weeks it is full grown. A dog after two years, or a horse after about five, are as much of a dog or a horse as they will ever be. It takes on an average twenty-one years for a child to become a man or a woman ; and even then sometimes it seems as if a few years more ripening would not do them much harm, but would make them all the more of a man or a woman. Nature never scamps her work, and she won't permit any one else to scamp it for her.

There is a story told of an ancient Greek who had a large number of bees. He noticed that they every day took a long and troublesome flight of many miles to Mount Hymettus, a mountain that was rich in flowers such as the bees love. He thought of a plan to save them the trouble of their tedious journey, and get a larger supply of honey for himself. He placed quite close to their hives a number of the finest flowers and then proceeded to cut their wings, so that they couldn't fly so far as before. It was a very clever idea. But unfortunately, when he had carried it out, the bees made no honey.

And as with bees, so with boys and girls. Young and old alike would do well to remember that there is no way of shortening the distance to man- and womanhood. If you try to curtail it, both your early and your later age will be a mistake. The gourd of the prophet Jonah grew up over night, and it perished over night. It came fast and went fast. Those who ripen too quickly, decay too quickly. Oh that it may be said of every one of you, for your own good of body and of soul, " The child was a child."

And, dear children, if you should think of being anything else, you will have not only Nature, but men also against you. There are few things more distasteful to people of sense and feelings than the sight of children who " ape " the manners of their elders. Why does the sight of an ape produce a more revolting feeling in us than that of many another animal ? Because the ape is so very much like a man without actually being one. The very likeness is the cause of disgust. The little would-be men and women arouse a feeling of something of the same kind ; perhaps mingled with pity and compassion, if their faults are unknown to themselves.

I do not know if there are among you any of what are called precocious children. If so I am very sorry for you. For a precocious child—that is, a child who has more of the man or woman in it, than of the boy or girl—may be the pride of foolish parents, he is the pain of all sensible strangers. I verily believe that there are few creatures more offensive than men-boys and women-girls. It was not so with the boy Samuel. Separated early in life from father and mother in order—such was the condition in those times—the better to serve his God and his people, living long among strangers, they learned to love him because he remained with all his gifts the child Samuel, until advancing years established him as a prophet and judge in Israel, whose fame spread from Dan to Beersheba. But meanwhile the child Samuel, as the Bible tells us,

S.C.   F

grew on, and was in favour both with the Lord and also with men.

Should you be desirous to know how you can best acquit yourselves in your own age, the answer lies in the words " The child was a child." Both before your fellow-men and before your God strive to be and to appear nothing but the children which you are. Be natural, be childlike, be yourselves. Get rid in the first instance of all assumptions and presumptions, of every particle of vanity, if vanity has once found a lodgment in your heart. It is sure to change your nature, and will unfit you to be men and women when your present age has long been left behind. I cannot too warmly impress upon my young hearers the duty of behaving themselves with modesty, with diffidence, and even with a certain amount of self-suspicion in their inter-course with their elders, their teachers and also with their companions. I have often heard it remarked that Jewish boys and girls behave rather more boldly than they should at school ; that they like to assert them-selves, and seem afraid people will not notice their merits enough. I do not know if there be any truth in all this. I am certain there should not be, for it is as utterly un-Jewish as it is unchildlike. It was not by clamour and by self-assertion that Samuel grew to be, and to be recognized as, a prophet in Israel.

And while you learn not to estimate yourselves too highly, learn not to estimate others too meanly. Learn to think and speak justly, kindly and even charitably of the world that is outside yourself. There is a habit that is springing up among many boys and girls—I wish it were repressed in elders—the habit of refusing to admire anything and anybody ; of despising or sneering at whatever comes under their notice ; of forming, even early in life, harsh and contemptuous and unkind judgments of other people's characters.   Avoid that habit. Shun it like the plague.   For if you do not, when you grow up men will shun you like a plague.   There is nothing manly or womanly about it, even if you wish to be men and women.   It is more than a fault, it is a vice that never takes root in the healthy nature of a true child.   A true child is one that has not lost faith in human goodness, and suspects no harm because it practises none.

So was it with Samuel.   Though the bearer of a divine message of punishment to Eli, he felt this child-like reluctance to think or speak harshly of others. " And he feared to tell Eli the vision."   Some children are very pleased when their elders make a mistake and give them a chance to correct them.   But Samuel could not bear to tell harsh and unpleasant things to Eli, and he only did so when he was very much pressed and urged by Eli himself to do so.

But there is something more to say, though I hope it will not make you feel conceited when I say it.   The child Samuel could hear a voice which Eli could not hear.   In the hearts of men and women there is often so much going on, such tumult and confusion ; conflicting passions strive for mastery, and in the noise and tumult the voice of God is not heard.   But in the heart of a true child there is silence and calm, and the voice of God makes itself heard.   It may sound so gently that it seems like a soft whisper in one's sleep ; it may be in the accents and the words of a beloved teacher, whose voice comes back to you, giving you good lessons how to be good.   You may always know that it is God's voice if it tells you, as the voice of God told Samuel, that doing wrong brings a punishment, that only by goodness can you be happy.

And when you hear such a voice may you always be ready to answer as Samuel answered : " Speak, Lord, for Thy servant heareth." May the Lord help you so to live that you be real, true children as long as you are children, and that when your childhood has passed, the innocence of childhood may not have vanished with it, and that from day to day, like another Samuel, you may grow before the Lord, ministering unto Him, and doing the work which He will one day expect of you all.

THE TABERNACLE

(*New West End Synagogue,*
Feast of Tabernacles, October 1st, 1898.)

LEVITICUS xxiii. 42, 43 : " Ye shall dwell in booths seven days ; all that are home-born in Israel shall dwell in booths : that your generations may know that I made the children of Israel to dwell in booths, when I brought them out of the land of Egypt."

HAVE you ever heard the story of Abbas, King of Persia, and the shepherd boy Ali ? Abbas the Great was King or Shah of Persia. One day he went out hunting and lost his way. Wandering about he came to a mountain, on whose side a shepherd was seated, watching his flocks, and amusing himself by playing the flute. The King went up to him and spoke to him. He found the boy a frank, intelligent, delightful lad, and took such a fancy to him that he got him to come and live with him at the royal court. As time went on, the boy Ali rose more and more in the King's favour. He worked hard ; he was clever ; he was true and faithful, and step by step was raised to the highest office of State— even to become the King's Treasurer. Always he remained honest and steadfast.

Shah Abbas died, and he was followed by a ruler, Shah Sefi, who was a very suspicious man. Ali's greatness got him many enemies ; people hated him because he succeeded so well, and they thought they would please the King and do themselves some little good by telling him all sorts of terrible things about the Treasurer, Ali. They said that he kept for himself a great deal of the money which ought to go to the King's treasury, and that his house was full of riches that were not honestly his. One day the King and his courtiers paid a surprise visit to the house of Ali ; they thought they would take the great minister unexpectedly and find out all about him. Well, it *was* a surprise visit, for the result was that it surprised the visitors very much. Instead of a magnificent palace with costly furniture and filled with precious things, they beheld a simple abode, fitted up in quite a humble manner. The King felt a little ashamed, and was obliged to confess to himself that the Grand Treasurer of his kingdom lived in a style no better than that of an ordinary citizen.

As he and his followers were going away, one of his courtiers drew the King's attention to a door at the end of a passage, a door which was double-bolted and barred. The King drew near and asked of Ali what it was he kept so safe behind those bars and bolts. Ali appeared shocked, he grew red in the face, but recovered himself and said, " Sire, in this apartment I keep the dearest thing I have in the world—my own property, my very own. All that thou hast seen in the house is my lord's, the King's ; this is mine alone. But it is a secret. I beg thee demand not to see it."

Well, you know what kings are—they are very much like boys and girls, the more you want to keep a thing from them, the more they want to know all about it. Besides, the Shah Sefi felt quite certain in himself that this mystery was a sign of Ali's guilt. So he ordered the door to be burst open, and they all entered the room, and what was it they beheld ? Four plain white walls, and hanging therefrom a shepherd's staff, a shepherd's flute, a shepherd's wallet or pocket, and an old garment; these were the treasures so firmly secured under iron bolts and bars.

Of course all present were very much surprised and more ashamed than ever, when Ali broke the silence and with perfect modesty said, " O King, when Abbas the Great first found me upon my mountain, feeding and guarding my flocks, these poor trifles were my only wealth. Since then I have guarded them as my true property, the memorials of my happy childhood. I trust your Majesty will not take them from me, but will permit me to return to those peaceful villages where in my poverty I was happier than I am in the splendour of thy court."

But the King took off his own royal mantle, and placed it upon Ali's shoulders, as a sign of the highest kingly favour.

Now, dear children, when we Jews keep the Festival of Tabernacles, when we go into a Succah, or little summer-house, and look at its frail roof of green twigs and leaves and think of what it all stands for, we do the very kind of thing which helps to remind us first of our humble beginning, and next of our wonderful history; only it is no secret. God, of course, knew that His people would not remain for all time a nation of wanderers. He knew that they would grow in number and in power, in riches ; He knew that great changes would come over them in the course of time ; that they would be scattered over the whole globe, and that they would be tempted to forget, and perhaps even to deny, all about their past history. And so He gave His Law, " All that are Israel, every native born in Israel, shall dwell in booths, in order that your generations may know that it was in booths I made the children of Israel to dwell when I brought them out of the land of Egypt." There we have the signs of what once we Jews were. We have got houses now, strong and walled, and well roofed; houses that protect us from the weather, full of comfort, and even of extra things called luxuries. But it is no disgrace, dear children, on the contrary, it is honourable to remember that it was not always thus. We do not mind if all the world knows that it was in booths that could be put up in a few hours and taken down in a few minutes that the race to which you and I belong spent their youth.

There is in the city of Frankfort a house in which the beginning was made of the fortune of a well-known family, celebrated not only for wealth but for charity. They have grown too large for the place, but they take care to keep the house up and to prevent it falling into decay. I have heard it said that there is an idea that if that house falls the family will fall. I should not like to answer for that ; but of this I am sure, that if we Jews were to do nothing to keep up the memory of our beginning, if we gave up keeping this festival of Tabernacles for instance, and other holy days and observances, it would not be long before we went to pieces. And that also is the meaning of the words, " Every one born in Israel shall dwell in booths, in order that your generations may know," i.e. the more careful every one of you is to keep up this sacred custom, the longer will your religion live, and generation after generation know how God made our fathers to dwell in booths while sojourning in the wilderness.

You see then, dear children, that one great lesson the Succah teaches us is to make us lowly and to keep us lowly before our God. Observing the festival regularly, year in year out, must help to do that. Some people remain humble enough while they are struggling for what they want, and when they have got all they want, they throw off all their lowliness and blossom out in pride and arrogance. In a poem by Browning—he is a writer whom children do not generally read, and not all grown-up people either—there is a capital story, in some ways like, but in the chief point very unlike, the Persian story with which I began. It is a story of a fisher-boy who became a Pope, the highest office you know which any one can reach in the Roman Catholic Church. Yes, he was the son of a poor fisherman, and he used to help his father with the nets with which the fish were caught. Well, he rose step by step from deacon to priest, from priest to bishop, from bishop to cardinal. And at all these stages he used to have put before him, so that all the world could see it as well as he himself, what do you think—the fishing net he used when a boy. He used to say :—

From fisher's drudge to Church's prince—it is indeed a rise ;
So here's the way to keep the fact for ever in my eyes.

Well, one day a new Pope had to be elected, and for this purpose it is always one of the Cardinals who is chosen, and the other Cardinals who choose him. They met together, and they all agreed that a man so lowly as the Cardinal who always kept before his view the sign of his station when he was a poor fisher-boy, he would make the best and most humble Pope. So they elected him, but no sooner was he made Pope than he had the net taken away from his presence. The others were all very much astonished, until at last one bolder than the rest asked him outright, " Father, why is the net removed ? " " Son," replied the Pope, " the net has caught the fish." You see he had gained all he wished for, and then all his humility was gone. There may be many who act like that.

But that is just what Jews must not do. God has been very good to us. The higher we rise the less our hardships become, the more prosperous we are, the more the honours and the pleasures of the world come to our share—and some or all of these may one day be yours—the more necessary is it for us to remember how simple were our beginnings, and to let the world know that nothing but a simple booth was our dwelling, under God's protection, when He brought us forth from Egypt—the more is it our duty to walk humbly with our God.

To be lowly with God, this is the first lesson the Succah teaches us. And the other is to be restful with God. When a child is asked, What did the Israelites do in the wilderness ? the answer generally is, They wandered about for forty years. Good gracious ! Have you ever thought what wandering about for forty years means ? It is a great mistake. A very large, perhaps the larger, part of the time they were not wandering, but just resting in their tented camp. We are told of long periods during which they had to remain encamped not only for a day or two, but for a month or a year it might be. What they learnt in the wilderness was not only to march and move, but to keep still—a much more difficult thing—to children as well as to grown-up people,—sometimes the most difficult thing in the world.

Now there is no doubt that restlessness is one of the principal faults of the time in which we live, and perhaps there was never so much of it as now. People want to do everything quickly ; they want to get on quickly, to become clever quickly, to grow rich quickly, to become men and women quickly. But God will not have it so, He wants us to hasten slowly ; and He says to us through the mouth of His servant, " Be still and know that I am God " ; and He teaches us in the history of our people that, even at the time when His great object was to lead our fathers into the promised land, He made them dwell in booths. Remember it was not by constant and restless marchings, nor even by making a sudden dash for the Holy Land, that we got it, but by first learning how to restrain ourselves, how to keep our souls in patience, as well as our bodies calm and restful.

And of course one thing led to another, by being restful in God we were restful and at peace with one another.

They lived then together, it would seem, in a friendly and affectionate way, each family in its own tabernacle. You might say, How do we know that they did get on so well with one another in their tents ? Well, I can't be absolutely certain about it, but I fancy if they had quarrelled we should have heard about it. In those days whenever the Israelites had to put up with anything unpleasant they always murmured, grumbled very loudly indeed ; but while we find them complaining about all sorts of things, objecting to this and to that, and especially so about being made to suffer any inconvenience, we never hear one word of complaint that their dwellings did not suit them. And so I think I am right in saying that in those days already there was strong family love among our people, and as God wanted it to continue and to be proved for age after age, He gave His command, " Ye shall dwell in booths for seven days."

When there is goodwill in a family there is space enough for them in a hut ; when there is no goodwill among them a palace is not large enough.

Be humble, be patient, be affectionate—those are some of the many lessons that the Tabernacle may teach us.

LIGHT

(*Great Synagogue, Children's Chanuka Service,*
December 17th, 1903.)

Psalm xviii. 29 : " For Thou wilt light my lamp, the Lord my
God will enlighten my darkness."

So King David prayed to God, and praised and thanked
Him after He had delivered him from the hands of all
his enemies. " For Thou wilt light my lamp." He
meant, of course, that God had taken care of him, had
protected him, had not allowed the light of his life, his
soul to be extinguished, and in the midst of the darkness of all his troubles had not only saved him, but had
made things clear to him that would have been dark to
others with less faith in God than King David.

There is a wonderful lot of meaning in a little light,
dear children, if we look at it not only with our eyes
but with our minds open. It does not matter what it
is. It may be of oil, or of wax, or gas, or electricity ;
it may be a torch, or a lamp, or a candle, or just a little
taper. That does not matter. All depends upon how
we look at it.

I am not speaking now of the way in which light acts,
though that is perhaps the most wonderful of all, how
it moves in immensely swift waves that strike a part of
the eye called the retina, and makes a picture on it, and
excites a certain nerve which carries a message to the
brain, and so that our *mind* sees as well as our *eye*. I

am thinking now rather of something else—I am thinking not of what light is, but of what light stands for.
For instance, light stands for rejoicing. You recollect
what happened when Haman's plans for crushing the
Jews were overthrown, and Mordecai and Esther saved
their people from destruction, how they celebrated
their deliverance ? The Jews, says the Bible, had
light, and joy, and gladness, and honour. Light and
gladness always go together among us. And you recalled, of course, what we do after some great victory, or
on Coronation Day, or the King's birthday. There is
always a grand illumination after dark, and all the chief
streets and buildings, and many of the little ones too,
blaze out in light ; for light means rejoicing.

Then again light stands for welcome. If you have a
friend or relation coming to see you, you light up an
extra candle or two or an extra jet of gas, to show that
you are glad to have them with you again. It is more
cheery and encouraging ; one feels that instinctively.
How do we welcome the Sabbath ? By special Sabbath
lights. That is how we honour the Sabbath, as though
she were a queen or a bride ; and right glad are we to
welcome and honour that blessed weekly visitor.

I have read of a poor old widow whose son once left
his home in a fit of anger and ill-temper. But the
mother, who had already forgiven him—as is the way of
mothers—before he had well crossed the threshold, but
who never knew where he had gone to, always expected
him back again, and not knowing whether it might not
be night when he returned, always before she went to
sleep o' nights put a lighted lamp in the window, so that
should he perchance return in the dark he might know
the old cottage again, and read in that steadily burning

light that threw its rays out into the dark night a sign that he was welcome and expected.

And then again light stands for guidance and caution. All round our coast, and especially in the more dangerous parts, there are beacons dotted about ; and each has its own way of signalling, which the mariners understand, and as the ships pass to and fro in the dark, the seamen can tell exactly where they are, and keep far away, especially in stormy weather, from the rocks or sandbanks on which otherwise they might founder. Those lights never fail to warn them and to direct them aright, and the same thing of course applies to railway signals.

And once more, light stands for hope and promise. When Columbus set out on his voyage to discover a new world, in which he believed, though neither he nor any man in Europe had ever seen it, he had to pass through a terrible time of discouragement. He had been beating about for many weeks upon the Atlantic ; and his crew were getting mutinous, and they wanted to force him to return. He was thinking of the jeers and jests with which he would be received if he came back with his task unfinished. Then one night as he was peering over the bows of the vessel he saw what appeared to him a tiny speck of light ; his heart beat high, he could hardly trust his eyes. He called his companions to give their opinion, and they too thought they saw the light. And though it soon disappeared the brave mariner kept on his course through the unknown seas, and when morning broke they found they were really drawing near to land. That light—perhaps from some humble fisherman's hut—was the first gleam of the New World. To it, and the promise it gave and the hope it kindled, we owe, in a certain sense, the discovery of America—a discovery that has done more than anything else during the last 400 years for the progress of the whole human race. So the light is what is called a symbol of hope and promise.

Light also stands for safety. In olden times when the streets had no lamps, and of course no electric light, people who were out at night carried lanterns with them to secure them against attacks. When they had lights they felt safe. Some little children, however, are very foolish to be afraid of the dark. Their mothers and fathers are watching over them, they never need be afraid. Mother and father go to sleep, too. But then there is God. He is always awake ; He never sleeps. He puts His watch-lights in the sky, the moon and stars, just as by day He sends the sunshine. Why, the sun is *always* shining somewhere ! Sometimes here, sometimes in Australia, but it never goes out. So all the world is safe, because there is light everywhere.

And light is a symbol of something more.

Those of you who have learned English history and have got as far as the reign of Queen Mary will remember how people were in those days burnt because there was some little difference between their religious belief and that of those who held power for the time being. Of course nowadays we should be ashamed to hurt other people because they don't believe as we do. But it was different then. Now when two good men, Bishops Latimer and Ridley, were led to the stake at Oxford, Latimer greeted the other with the words : " Be of good comfort, Master Ridley, and play the man ; we shall this day light such a candle by God's grace in England as (I trust) shall never be put out."

So the light stands as a memorial of martyrs, of good and great men who gave up their lives for what they believed true, and thus have left to succeeding ages the bright light of their noble example that will never, never be extinguished.

Now we have just looked on while the Chanuka lights have been kindled. Do you know, dear children, that every one of those lessons to which I have just referred, every one of them is taught us by those lights, and even more if we had time to dwell upon them.

Those lights are a memorial of the brave men and women who died for the sake of their religion in those stirring days of Mattathias and Judas the Maccabee. They were the very first martyrs who gave up their life for Judaism. There have been many since, more in proportion to their numbers among Jews than among any other people on the face of the earth. But the noble Maccabees, men and women, old and young, were the first, and surely we do well to keep the memory of them bright by kindling these memorial lights on our Festival of Chanuka. There are a couple of beautiful lines in Shakespeare's *Merchant of Venice*, which, if you have not yet learned, I hope you soon will :—

> How far that little candle throws his beams!
> So shines a good deed in a naughty world.

Those lights are a message too of hope and promise to us all, to all who remain steadfast in doing their duty. They tell us not to despair when we are in darkness and tossed about on a sea of troubles, that all things will come right if we have a good cause and believe in it and steadily and hopefully follow it.

And they are to serve as a guide and as a caution to

us. In the days of Antiochus and the Maccabees there were some in Israel who allowed themselves to be drawn out of the path of their pure religion by the attractions and the idolatries of the Greeks and Syrians. They went about the business of their lives carelessly, thoughtlessly, heartlessly ; they paid no heed to the warning beacons set up by the Law of God ; and, behold, they were swallowed up by the enemy, lost in the great multitude, their very names forgotten or remembered only for "shame." Surely we shall take warning by them.

And these lights are a symbol of safety to us. While we keep them alight, while we are full of brave determination to fight with all our might for what we feel to be the truth, we are safe. God is with us, for we are with Him ; and when *He* is with us, what have we to fear ?

These lights, too, serve as a sign of welcome to us. For, dear children, you are all most welcome here to-day, you little know how welcome. Yours is a religion that loves to see its children caring for the old faith. And even—though I trust this will never be the case— even if you should stray away from it for a while, it will gladly have you back again, though you need not wait for another Chanuka for this, for you know there is always one light kept burning in every synagogue, the "perpetual light," as a sign that you are welcome and expected at any time.

But above all remember that these lights are kindled to express the gratitude and the gladness of our hearts for all that God has done for us and for our fathers. Yours is a religion that loves you to be happy. You cannot please God more than by a bright and cheerful spirit. "Serve the Lord with gladness ; " you cannot serve Him to any good purpose properly except in gladness.

And thus doing your part you may each rest on God. And doing so you may confidently turn to God and pray with the Psalmist, " For Thou wilt light my lamp, the Lord my God will enlighten my darkness."

Almighty God, we thank Thee for this happy festival, and for the glorious memories it brings to our minds, and for the brave and good men and women and children whom Thou didst raise up in the days of old. Help us to be like them, to be good and brave, to be true to Thy Law, and to live by it and for it. Put light into all hearts to-day. And even as these festive lights grow in number day by day, so may we also day by day grow in knowledge and in goodness, in gratitude to Thee, in love and respect for our parents and teachers, and in loving-kindness to all our fellow-beings. And as Thou didst of old choose Israel to be a light to all nations on earth, may we by being faithful to Thee, bring illumination to all men, so that in Thy light we and they may see light for ever.

SHORT AND LONG WAYS

*(New West End Synagogue,
Passover, April 15th, 1887.)*

EXODUS xiii. 17, 18 : " And it came to pass, when Pharaoh
had let the people go, that God led them not by the way of the
land of the Philistines, because that was near ; for God said,
Lest the people repent when they see war, and they return to
Egypt : but God led the people about by the way of the wilderness by the Red Sea."

LET us begin with a story from one of the rabbinical
books.   A stranger is approaching Jerusalem and meets
a boy, of whom he asks the shortest way to the city.
" This way," said the boy, pointing in one direction, " is
short and long ; that other is long and short."   The
traveller chooses the first road, and in a very short time
comes in sight of the holy city, but advancing, he finds
that the city is surrounded with fields and gardens,
which he is obliged to avoid, and so goes to and fro until
he is quite exhausted without having yet reached the
place for which he started.   Seeing again the boy who
had directed him, he addresses him very angrily and
says : " Did you not tell me that road was the short
one ? "   " Yes," returned the lad, " and long too.
You ought to have taken the other, then you would have
been there by this time."

Now I fancy, dear children, that some of you in your
wanderings, whether in town or country, have dis-

covered something of the same sort. A way appears short and enticing, and you follow it only to find that it proves long and wearisome, and your experience may sometimes teach you that the road which looks the farthest and most trying is really the nearest and easiest. The fact is you must use your judgment as well as your eyes in these matters, and if you do not you may bring no small amount of trouble on yourself.

Of course when God chooses the road for us, and directs us in the way in which we should walk, we are in no danger of going wrong. Be it the shortest or be it the longest, it is certainly the best. And this brings us to the sacred words with which our Scripture lesson began this morning.

The people of Israel were free at last; they were not merely allowed to go, they were driven forth from Egypt. Now came the question, what use were they to make of their freedom? It might prove a blessing, and it might prove a bane to them. They had set out with the object of finding a resting place for themselves in the land promised to their fathers. The straightest route leading from Egypt to Palestine runs in a north and north-easterly direction, and would have occupied a space of about ten days. But suppose they had travelled in that direction, what would have happened? They would have met a strong and warlike race, and, themselves new and untrained to warfare, the chances were that they would have lost heart at the first encounter, and so have undone all that had at present been effected for their good. They would have fled back to Egypt, have put themselves under their old masters, and been in a worse state than ever. The work of deliverance would have had to be done all over again. This way, then—the way by the land of the Philistines—looks short, but it would have been very long.

And so we see that one reason why the Israelites were not led along the nearest route to their land was the tender and loving consideration of God for the weakness of His people. He did not expect from a nation just in possession of their liberty what He might look for from an army of veteran soldiers. He therefore spared them a trial which He knew was too much for their strength.

If you will look about you in your own little world a bit, I think you will find God still at work just in the same way. He does not ask of men nowadays what only angels could perform, and He does not ask of you children what only men and women used to the battle of life could do. There is a famous saying that " God tempers the wind to the shorn sheep." He seems to make things not light for us to bear, but just heavy enough for our strength. Consider how, in your own lives, dangers to which you prove unequal are kept far from you. From how much trouble and anxiety are you screened, be it through the direct goodness of God or through that parental love which is the nearest to God's love of all the feelings that find room in the human heart. If there is a sorrow in your house, you are the last to hear of it; if there is cause for rejoicing, you are the first to share it. You are spared whatever might tax your strength over much, so that you might not lose heart on your first acquaintance with life. And not against bodily harm alone are you guarded with a wise and watchful care ; there are worse evils that threaten us than any affliction that can befall this body of ours. From all unholy and degrading thoughts, even as far as possible from vicious and harmful ex-

ample, more contagious than any disease, and more to
be dreaded than any foe, you are protected and have
been from your infancy. God in His wisdom knows
that such things would effectually stop your way to your
Holy Land, and He saves you in His mercy from the
sorrow and the ruin that might otherwise be your fate,
even in the early days of your life.

But now I want you to notice another and not less
important point. Not only does God not lead the
children of Israel by the near way through the Philistine
country, but He seems to avoid it *because it was* near.
Some translators render the words, "*although* it was
near." He did not lead them through the Philistine
land " although it was near." But this Hebrew word
seldom means *although*, and almost always *because*, and
does so in the same verse again, " *because* God said lest
the people be sorry," when they see the enemy in front of
them and run back to Egypt. So that it would appear as
if God avoided that route through the Philistine country
just because it was near, for of course He might have
conquered the enemy by a miracle, only you must bear
in mind that God never has recourse to miracles when
the ordinary means at hand are sufficient for His purpose. Well, instead of taking them by the nearest way,
He seems rather to shun it because it is the nearest, and
to take them by the farthest. " God made them go
about by the way of the wilderness and the Red Sea," as
you might see if you will examine any map of those
parts.

And why all this ? Because, as we now know, it was
in God's plan to train the people whom He had delivered
to become a kingdom of priests and a holy nation, and
that couldn't be done in a week or two ; because He had

in store for them many a precious treasure for which they would probably have cared but little had they become quickly possessed of fields and vineyards ; because a period of discipline was needed to teach the people of Israel, if it was possible to teach them, how to value their many blessings and how to use the powers God had entrusted to them. And just as Moses, their inspired leader, had spent forty long years of thought and toil in the desert before he was fit to become their deliverer, so now commenced another such period of forty years of wandering and trial, learning and reflection and action, for the people whom he had freed from slavery to make them fit to enter and take possession of the country promised to their forefathers. It might seem the longer way of reaching the Holy Land, but it was certainly the safer way of getting there, and the surer way of staying there. Hundreds of years later, one of the Psalmists, referring to this very event, said, " He led them forth by the right way, that they might go to a city of habitation " (Ps. cvii. 7).

And this is the second lesson which I hope you will take away with you to-day. We are not called into this world, any of us, to have things made nice and easy for us. If God saves us from trials that would be likely to crush us, He doesn't save us from those that ought only to strengthen us. He loves us, like a wise parent, that is, too much to spoil us. For us also the longest and most trying way may prove the best in the end.

Depend upon it, dear children, if any work of ours is to live and bear good fruit in the world, it is that which has cost us time and care. No power on earth can save us from either, or would be our friend if it could and did save us. A great German poet chose as his motto,

" Ohne Hast, ohne Rast "—" Unhasting, unflagging."
It is a perfect picture of the way in which all the noblest
lives have been lived, " unhasting, unflagging."

You may take it for granted that there are no short
cuts to anything worth having. There are no short
cuts to fortune or to learning, or to anything else men
prize. Take, for instance, the people who are in a hurry
to get rich. Money is their promised land, and they
think they can get it by making a dash ; but they have
unfortunately taken no sufficient account of the enemy,
and perhaps at the very moment when they believe
themselves secure in what they have obtained by bold-
ness and luck, they are driven back, and baffled and
beaten they return to a worse condition than ever they
were in before.

Or do you think that knowledge can be got by any
short cut, by any patent process ? Not a bit of it ;
nothing but the patient pursuit of it, over hill and dale,
through streams and deserts, will be rewarded with
success. Many people nowadays fancy they have
discovered the means of getting the largest knowledge
with least amount of trouble. But it all comes to
nothing, or worse. The old way is the only safe way :
" Line upon line, line upon line ; here a little, there a
little." In fact learning always avenges herself on the
man who plays tricks on her, by making a fool of him.

It is a law of human nature, too, that whatever we
get very easily we value but slightly. Whatever we get
too quickly we shall lose too quickly. See what happens
in nature : the wood that grows the quickest splits the
easiest, that which grows the slowest is the hardest. It
is so also in all mechanical arts of man. If you build a
house too rapidly, before the mortar has time to settle,

it will bulge and tumble in. If you want the house to hold out, so must you. It is so in all the higher efforts in which we should engage. One has to learn an enormous quantity before one knows a very little. Some one was praising a work of Sir Joshua Reynolds one day. " That's a splendid picture of yours," he said. " One picture ? " Sir Joshua replied ; " it is ten pictures." The artist had to paint it and repaint it before he reached the ideal he had placed before him. So, too, an eminent preacher was asked how long it took him to prepare a sermon of his which had made a very deep impression on his hearers. " Forty years."

It is no doubt very pleasant if you can be a great genius ; but geniuses are very few, and even they are mostly men and women gifted with an endless capacity for taking pains. The celebrated Dr. Arnold once said : " If there be one thing on earth truly admirable, it is to see God's wisdom blessing an inferiority of natural powers, when they have been honestly, truly and zealously cultivated." Speaking on one occasion of a pupil of this kind, he said, " I would only stand to that man hat in hand." Yes, dear children, there is but one true way to success in life—it is the long and sometimes hard and trying way—where we must be prepared to work steadily onwards and upwards, and not only to work, but to suffer failure and disappointment without losing sight of the object for which we started. For if you try, you have succeeded ; trying is success. A Rabbi said : " If any one tells me he found anything without troubling to look for it, I do not believe him ; nor would I believe him if he say, I took trouble to look for the thing, but did not find it." It is the trouble you take that means everything ; whether you obtain what the world calls success or suffer what the world calls failure—so long as you have done your best you have won what God wishes you to win, you have done what He sets you to do.

And if what I said just before is true of what is done by the human intellect—I mean if it is only by trying, by slow effort that anything can be done—it is true in a still stronger sense of what is to be done by the human heart. You see we have not only a mind to cultivate, but a character to train. Here especially the process must be a long and trying one. God leads us about by the way of the wilderness and the sea. For the purpose of bringing to light whatever is good in us the short and easy way, or the way which would require that God should do all the work and we nothing, would not answer at all. You know that among the wonders of our time are the immense quantity and variety of machines that have been and are being invented, to do by mechanical means the work that would otherwise have to be done by men or animals. People speak of them as " labour saving apparatus." But no ingenuity has ever yet invented " labour saving " engines for the human character. Every bit of the work has to be done by our own hands or it is not done at all ; every bit of the road has to be travelled on foot or we shall never get along at all. Good men and women, above all good Jews and Jewesses, are not made by shirking trials, but by bearing them and triumphing over them.

And this, I trust, dear children, will be the task to which you will betake yourselves, the road along which you will travel. Do not flatter yourselves that you will escape your share of hardships or of temptations in the journey that lies before you, but strive to be prepared for them—welcome even in your youth that discipline which loving hearts impose upon you, because they know what is in store for you ; look forward to your future full of trust in Him who directs your path. On your part be strong and of a good courage, and you will find that there is One who will not suffer your foot to stumble, for your Heavenly Guardian slumbereth not.

THE SOUL

(New West End Synagogue,
Passover, 1906.)

PSALM lxvi. 16 : " Come and hear, all ye that fear God, and I will declare what He hath done for my soul."

YOU will, I think, have understood a good deal of this beautiful psalm.   You will notice that it is a call to all people to join in thankfulness for what God has done for them.   The Psalmist thinks also of the trials through which they have passed—in ancient times when God turned the sea into dry land for them, and in later days when He held their souls in life.   He remembers the troubles they had to bear, and how they were delivered from them all.   But he is not satisfied with talking about other people and pointing out their duties to them. He delights to think of his own history, and of his own duties ; especially does he exult to tell of God's peculiar mercies to him personally, or, as he expresses it, to declare what God has done for his soul.

This last thought I would ask you, dear children, to fix a little more clearly in your minds, and to see how such words might be made to apply to you. " Come and hear, all ye that fear God, and I will declare to you what He hath done for my soul."

A beautiful story is related in connexion with the late Emperor Frederick of Germany, who is often spoken of and with reason as Frederick the Good. He once visited a school and asked the children how many kingdoms there are. A little girl answered : " There are four : the mineral kingdom, the vegetable kingdom, the animal kingdom, and the kingdom of God."

The child who spoke thus in the innocence of her heart must have herself been of the kingdom of God, and the truth she expressed, perhaps knowing only a very small part of what it meant, is precious for you also and for all creatures who have a soul. For it is that soul which distinguishes you from the mineral, from the plant, and from the rest of the animal world, you and such as you belong to the kingdom of God.

This, then, is the thing God has done for you more than for the rest of His creation ; He has given you a soul.

But you ask, " What is the soul ; what does it do ? " Of these questions it is not so easy to answer the first, " What is the soul ? " as the second, " What does it do ? " It is by what it does that you may know the soul. It is that within you which thinks and feels, and knows right from wrong, and believes in truth and goodness and in God, and, what is more, can think about all these things—namely, about thinking, and feeling, and knowing and believing. That is what the soul does. Whether dogs and other animals have a soul or not we cannot say. Certainly, if they have it is very, very different in kind to the human soul.

But what is the soul ? What is its nature ? Well, dear children, that is so difficult to understand that it is better to rest satisfied for the present with finding out what it is *not*. It is not *matter* ; it is not body. You are made up of two things, of matter and spirit, or of body and soul, of something visible and of something invisible. But, curiously enough, that which you can see is not nearly of so much consequence as that which you cannot see, for when the part you cannot see leaves you the other part corrupts and decays and moulders away.

Nay, when we get to think of it (as Armstrong points out) the matter that helps to make up a child or a man is not the man himself or the child himself at all. It is only something that *belongs* to the man or child—it is *his*, it isn't *he* ; it is his, like his clothes or his books or his tools. The real child or man is the *soul*, that which thinks and feels, and knows right from wrong, and can choose to do right and to be good if he pleases.

If I say I am cold, I mean that my hands or feet are cold ; if I say I am in pain, I mean that my head aches or my limbs ; if I cut myself and say " I am bleeding," I mean that my finger is bleeding. It isn't really *I* who am cold, or in pain, or bleeding, but my body, or part of it. The *feelings* connected with all these things belong to the soul, but not these things themselves.

But when I say, " I think this or that," " I know to-day is Passover" ; or when I say, " I hate," " I love," " I fear," " I hope," " I will do this or will not do that," then it is the real *I* that is meant—it is the soul that thinks and knows, hates and loves, fears and hopes and wills. It is certainly not my hands, or my head, or my body.

This then is the soul which God has given us. But God has done more for us than give us this soul. In that soul He is constantly speaking to us—He warns us against evil, He exhorts and encourages us to good. A boy, say, has done another a bad turn. The one who has been wronged is brooding over his wrongs, when suddenly he learns something very ill about his companion, the knowledge of which will do him immense damage. He will have his revenge he thinks; but while he is comforting himself in this way, a voice is heard, soft but most persistent, saying to him, "It is a mean thing that which you have in mind to do; it is a cruel thing, don't return blow for blow, leave him to his thoughts, keep your own unstained." That is the voice of God in your soul trying to give strength and health to your soul. Or you are out somewhere bent upon your own amusement, when you see some sad accident happen. Your first impulse after you have gratified your curiosity is to go after your own pleasure, shut from your mind the thought of the sufferings of others, and just follow the rule "everybody for himself." But then you hear another voice saying, "What are the pleasures you may give up compared with the suffering you might help to relieve? Come, make some sacrifice for the good of others, and don't think all your time and money misspent because it isn't spent upon yourself." That too is the voice of God in your soul, urging you on to be unselfish and merciful.

Then God has done something else for your soul. For not only does *He* speak to *you* through it, but *you* speak to *Him*, in prayer, And of all prayers that go up to Him, not one is as dear as the sweet, innocent prayers of children. If at night before going to sleep you pray, "O Lord God of my fathers, let me lie down in peace, and rise up in peace; into Thy hand I commend my spirit. O preserve my dear ones";—if in the morning you pray, "I thank Thee that Thou hast restored my soul to me in Thy great faithfulness. Teach me to love what is good and true, and help me to know and to do my duty to every one," or words to that effect, be sure the message is carried straight to God, for the soul of a good child is a faithful messenger, and, perhaps because it has not been long away from home, knows its way there so easily, and returns to tell you, " Verily God hath heard me, He hath attended to the voice of my prayer."

There is a little boy I know who does not always remember to say his prayers. His mother said to him one day : " How is it that you sometimes forget your prayers in the morning, but you never forget your breakfast ? " And the boy answered : " Because something inside me tells me that I want my breakfast, but nothing inside me reminds me of my prayers." His mother thought about that a good deal, and taught him more and more about the goodness of God and how much every one has to be thankful for ; taught him what God wants of every little boy and girl, taught him to sing psalms and to love his prayers ; in fact she educated his soul. Then it was not long before he felt something hurting him inside when he forgot his prayers : it hurts more than hunger when once you get to feel that pain ; and when you satisfy that inward craving, when you say your prayers, you feel full of love for God and your parents and companions, you feel strengthened and braced up for the day's work ; you overflow with happiness.

God has done something for your soul, dear children, which surpasses all His other gifts. He has taught us how to use it, how to train it, how to improve it and to fit it not only for a good and happy life here, but for a glorious and blissful life hereafter. He has left us in no doubt whatever as to the way in which this may be

S.C. H

brought about. In His book He has laid down exactly
how we are to act, what we must do and what leave
undone, in order that our soul may go from strength to
strength until we appear before the Lord in His Holy
Place in Heaven. He has not indeed described to us
what that Heaven is like, for we shouldn't understand
it, if we had been told, and we should only worry ourselves because of lack of power to understand it, and
that is why one of the prophets so wisely said, " No eye
but Thine, O Lord, hath seen that which Thou hast
prepared for him that hopeth for Thee"; but He has
made the road to the better land so clear to our souls
that no one who follows it can miss his way, though the
other world be all unknown to him.

But you ask : " How can you show that the soul can
live when it parts from the body. We only see them
together." Well, dear children, let us try to make it
clearer to ourselves by a couple of illustrations.

When the Spaniards first came among the poor
Indians, and having landed their horses rode on them,
the Indians, not knowing any better, thought that the
horse and his rider were one. So are there people who
fancy the body and the soul are one. But we know
that the horse may be killed under a man, and he yet be
perfectly free to move about as and where he likes.
And so, though the body perish that for a time supports
the soul, the soul may be free to move and think and will
as it pleases.

A teacher was once trying to explain to a number of
children that their souls would live after they were dead.
They listened, but evidently didn't understand ; so he
hit upon this plan to make it clear to them. Snatching
his watch from his pocket, he said, " James, what is this

I hold in my hand ? " " A watch, sir." " You all see it ? " " Yes." " How do you know it is a watch ? " " It ticks." He then took off the case, and held the case in one hand and the works in his other. " You see there are now two watches. Which ? " After a little hesitation : " The littlest one in your right hand." " Very well, but how do you know ? " " It ticks." " Very well again. Now I will lay aside the case—down, down in my hat. Now let us see if you can hear the watch tick." " Yes, sir, we hear it," exclaimed several voices. " Well, the watch can tick and keep time, you see, when the case is taken off and put away. So is it with you ; your body is nothing but the case, the soul is inside. The case, the body, may be taken off and buried in the ground, and the soul will live and think, just as well as this watch will go, as you see, when the case is off." It was one of the youngest children who went off and told his mother that his little soul would tick when he was dead.

But, you say, you are talking of life after death. How can there be such a thing ? I don't know how. I only know that you might ask a much more difficult question, How is it that the soul lives at all ? Yet it does. Why, then, should it not live again ? Which is more difficult, for something which has not existed before to exist now, or for something which exists now to exist again ? Now that is just what happens with the soul. There was a time when you were not in existence. God created a soul for you, He fashioned it exactly to your needs and put it into you. Well, He takes it from this world ; but is it not easier to make that soul live again than to make it live at all ?

People say, " But we have never known such a thing

as a soul having another life." That is quite true, and only shows that people do not know everything, and it is well that they should not know everything. But suppose a person to have been locked up in prison since his birth, and then one day to be set free, and to go out into the fields and forests when all the flowers were in bloom and the trees rich in foliage, and suppose he then watched the changes that take place in all the plant world, and to see all their beauty and glory decay and fall, and the stalks of the flowers wither away and the trees standing bleak and bare in the winter. Might not such a person say, " It is all over with them ; they are dead, they will never come to life again " ? For *he* had never known the like to happen. Yet *we*, who have seen Nature for more than six months, know that the trees and flowers do come to life again. What must have been the terror of Adam when for the first time he saw the sun set, and darkness spread over all the world ? How could he know that God would roll away the darkness from before the light ? And, dear children, " If light can thus deceive, wherefore not life." After all, the longest life is but a few summers and winters ; a pitiable small number of days compared with His whose years have no end. Let us be careful then in deciding what may or may not happen in a future of which we cannot form the dimmest notion from our past experience, and which is in the hands of the God of the spirits of all flesh.

Do not believe that God would spend so much wisdom and power and goodness in making and fitting out a human soul merely to let it live a few years and then to put it out as a candle is put out. No, it departs from here and may go, we know not where ; but He who takes care that the sun does not go out, even when it does not shine on us, will take care also that our light is not extinguished, even when it is removed from this portion of God's world.

So may all of you, dear children, believe, and in accordance with that belief may you live and act, and on His part may the Lord bless you and keep you; may the Lord make His countenance to shine on you and be gracious unto you ; may the Lord turn His face unto you and give you peace, now and for evermore.

ON TAKING CARE

(*New West End Synagogue,
Passover, April 6th,* 1904.)

DEUTERONOMY vi. 12 : " Take care thou forget not the Lord Who brought thee out of the land of Egypt, out of the house of bondage."

Do you know, dear children, that the Hebrew word for " take care " occurs over and over again in the Bible. I began to count the number of times it is used, but after about fifty I had to give it up. It is quite certain that Moses and the other great and good men who wrote the Bible would not have said so often " take care, take care," unless they had thought that there was a great deal in " taking care."

Now there are two kinds of care. There is the care which means worry and anxiety and sorrow. No human being can go through life quite free from it ; but we trust you will not have any of it for ever so long ; all who love you do what they can to keep it from you ; in fact they have the care so that you may be spared it. But there is another kind of care, which means being watchful and attentive, taking trouble about things, not being negligent and forgetful, not indulging yourself, and no one who really, wisely loves you would spare you that sort of care.

I have heard of a kind but not very wise mother who took her boy to a public school. She saw the head master, and said to him that her boy was a remarkable boy, but quite different from other boys. It was a Jewish mother and son, and she informed the master that her son was a perfect genius. But he was peculiar. He wasn't to be forced to do anything against his will ; not even to play. He was *such* a sensitive boy, and was on no account to be punished. " You want to save him from pain ? " " Yes," she said. " Well," replied the master, " this is an institution where the boys either take pains or they have pains given to them. Your son must make up his mind which he prefers. Otherwise he must try some other establishment."

And the same is true of everything in life, from our earliest to our latest days. If we don't take care, we shall have to suffer care ; if we won't take pains, we shall have them given us. I am sure I need not ask you which you prefer. " Take care that thou forget not."

There is a charming book which all boys and girls, of whatever age, should read. It is called Wood Magic, and was written by a man named Richard Jefferies. There is a squirrel in it and a delightful little boy named Bevis. And the squirrel teaches the little boy a lot of things, some of which I will tell you, though not always in the squirrel's exact words. Everything in the world says to us, Take care. For instance, Be very careful, Bevis dear, how you climb a tree, or how you bend out of window, for there is something at the bottom that is always lying in wait, and will pull you down in a minute if you don't take care. You can not see it, but it is there, as you can prove if you only let your cap go from the window or the tree.

Also you have seen people swimming, which is a very pleasant thing ; but they must take care that they don't stop swimming ; if they stop for a minute or so they will be drowned. And although a man soon gets tired of

swimming, the water never gets tired of waiting, but is
always ready to drown him.

Also, it is the same with your candle. There was
once a lady who used to go to bed and leave a lighted
candle in her room, and the candle would burn down to
the socket and then go out, and everything was all right.
But once she brought a pair of gloves home in a paper
parcel. And she took the gloves out, left the paper on
her dressing-table, and put the candle on it : and the
candle was stuck in the candlestick with some matches
to make it firm. And in the night, when she had fallen
asleep, the candle burnt down, and when the flame reached
the matches, it set them alight and when they had burnt
a little way down a bit fell off, and dropped on the piece
of paper. And the paper, being very thin, was alight
in an instant, and from the paper the flame spread to
some gauzy things that were round the lady's looking-
glass, and from there to the window curtains, until the
whole room was in a blaze. And the lady did not awake
until she was very much hurt.

Therefore, says the squirrel to Bevis, if you climb a
tree, be sure to remember to hold on ; for the earth will
not forget, and will pull you down with a thump, and
hurt you very much. And when you walk by the water,
do not forget it is water ; for the water won't forget, and
if you fall in, it will let you sink. And if you take a candle,
be careful what you are doing, and do not forget that the
fire will burn ; for the fire never forgets, but is always on
the look-out and ready, and will burn you without mercy.

And so everything in Nature says, Take care. Not
that these are bad things in themselves. On the contrary.
But for fire and water and gravitation we should not
exist.

Now, in this as in so many other things, the Bible says the same as Nature. " Take care, lest thou forget." So much suffering is caused in the world both to ourselves and others just for want of a little thought, just because we took no heed of what we had ourselves learned or what others from their experience have taught us.

But the Bible goes further and says, " Take heed lest thou forget the Lord "—the worst of all forgettings.

Take care thou forget not the Lord. It is very necessary to warn us of this, for there are some who do forget Him, it may be because they are so taken up with bothering themselves that they seem not to think about Him at all ; it may be that they are so taken up with enjoying themselves that they forget all about Him. A true Jew will not let either keep God out of his mind—and what is more, he will do what is right, not because that will lead to something pleasant, and he will avoid what is wrong ; not because he is afraid that it will lead to something unpleasant ; but he will do it for God's sake ; he will cease to do evil, he will learn to do good, because God has commanded it.

It is related in the Talmud that a certain Rabbi was once in Rome. While he was there the wife of the Emperor lost some valuable jewels. A proclamation was made that whoever found them and returned them before the lapse of thirty days should be handsomely rewarded ; but that after thirty days the finder, should he become known, should lose his head. Well the Rabbi (Samuel the son of Sisretai was his name) found them ; but he took no notice of the proclamation. After the month he went to the Empress and gave her back her lost jewels. " What meanest thou by such conduct ? " she said to him. " Madam," he replied, " I did not return them during the period fixed, that thou shouldst not think it was either hope of reward or fear of punishment from thee that prompted me. I have waited until now to return these jewels for God's sake, for the love and reverence of Him alone." Then the empress broke forth in words of praise of that God, saying, " Blessed be the God of the Jews."

Now I would not advise you, if you should be so fortunate as to find the Queen's jewels, or anybody else's— I would not advise any of you to wait thirty days before returning them. What you should do is to take them to a place called Scotland Yard, where the Lost Property Office is, or to the nearest police station. But I trust that you would do this, not from hope of reward, nor through fear of punishment, but because you are Jews and Jewesses, whom God has chosen to be an example to the world of all that is honourable, and who have been taught " Take care lest thou forget the Lord who brought thee out of the land of Egypt." For that is the greatest duty of all for us Jews.

And yet we are all of us very weak creatures—so apt to forget unless there is something actually before us, something to see, and to do, and to take part in, with our mind and heart, that shall prevent us forgetting. God knows this, and that is why he commanded us to keep the Passover seven days. Why ?

Even those we love and have reason to love we are likely to forget if we never see them, or speak to them, or write to them, or do something for them. And so with our whole history as Jews. If it had merely been put down in a book it would soon have been forgotten, but it is a holy day like this which comes round every year, for which we have to do something, to make some preparation, on which we eat unleavened bread, to come expressly to Synagogue—it is a day like this that keeps our memories ever fresh and green about what happened to our fathers : how once they were slaves, and how through the goodness of God they became free. So long as we keep Passover we never, never can forget Him who brought us forth out of the house of bondage. It is good for young and old. It is good for the simplest child, it is good for the wisest man and woman. It is all brought back to us in so lively a way : the hardship, and the gloom, and the promise, and those faithful servants of God—Moses and Aaron, and the divine help, and the crossing of the Red Sea, and the song of triumph and of thanksgiving. All this you must ever treasure in your memories. "Take care lest you forget."

DISCIPLINE

(*New West End Synagogue,*
Seventh day of Passover, April 23rd, 1897.)

PSALM CV. 37 : " And there was not one that stumbled among his tribes."

ONE of the most remarkable things about the departure from Egypt—I wonder whether it has ever struck you ? —is this fact, that all the Israelites, great and small, young and old, the strong and the feeble, all came away at a given hour of a given night, not one of them, not as much as a beast of theirs, being left behind. It was all done in a quiet and orderly fashion, so that before their enemies had recovered from the blow which fell upon them, the Israelites were already a long way off on the road to Sinai and to freedom. In itself perhaps it is not so very wonderful. People who have travelled and seen a great deal in the East tell us that it is a not at all uncommon thing for large masses of pilgrims, forming what are called caravans, to break up their encampment suddenly and quickly, and in the silence and cool of the night, with torches flaming before them, and a train of camels and asses spreading far and wide, to cross a huge stretch of the desert.

But in the first place our fathers were not used to that sort of life, and in the West, I am afraid it must be confessed, Israelites have always been very hard to manage. They never liked doing exactly as they were told, no matter who told them. Besides there was another great cause of confusion. There were a large number of boys and girls among them ; and again I am afraid it must be admitted that as a rule Jewish boys and girls are more difficult to manage than others. Whatever be the reason, whether Jewish parents love their children not always wisely but too well, or that the children have as is said such wonderful spirits, the fact remains that among those wonderful spirits the spirit of orderliness, of regularity, of ready obedience, all that makes up what is called discipline, is not always present.

All the more remarkable is it that on that memorable occasion which is recalled to our minds by this Festival of Passover, the Israelites of all ages and classes worked together with promptitude, with energy, with a good will, that may well serve as a lesson for us all. There were none that stumbled in all their tribes ; there were none that pushed too far and fast ahead, and got into mischief that way ; there were none that straggled and lagged behind, and got into mischief that way ; there were none that fell out on the line of march—all kept firmly and steadfastly together ; and so it came about that by this great effort of discipline, among young and old alike, the Israelite of that day first served himself, next served his brethren, and lastly served God.

Let me say a few words to you on each of these points. You serve yourself in the first instance, and you serve yourself most by every act of discipline, by every attempt to be master of yourself, to conquer your little faults and weaknesses. " There was not one that stumbled among his tribes." Now I fancy I hear some of my wiser hearers say, What merit is there in that ? A person stumbles because he cannot help it. If he could help it, he would not stumble. People who argue like that will, unless they alter their ways, never be able to walk straight and steady at all. We have got to make up our minds that stumbling is just one of the things we can help.

We are put into this world not to totter about, but to learn to be firm of foot and steady of step. From the time of our earliest childhood, from the first instant when we can feel and think, or at least when we can remember anything at all, we are all being taught that many things which seem to be *beyond* our power are really *in* our power. A very little child can only make meaningless noises and utter sounds without sense. But it is soon able to form those sounds into intelligible words. It does this by learning to control and discipline its tongue. So with singing. You will sometimes hear it said: So and so has not a very good voice but how well she sings! Training and discipline have turned a poor gift into a beautiful accomplishment. How do people learn to play the violin ? By practising. Now practising is only discipline; discipline of fingers, of ear, of taste. All, or nearly all our good habits, come from good order and discipline just as our bad habits come from bad order and want of discipline.

This is true of more important things than singing and violin playing. Our passions and temptations, our neighbours and companions, our troubles and our pleasures— all are meant as means of discipline for us, and if we know how to use them rightly will in the end benefit us.

The words just before the text are very curious. The whole verse thus runs : " He brought them out with silver and gold, and there was not one that stumbled among His tribes." You remember, of course, how our fathers when they left Egypt took with them much silver and gold from the Egyptians, which they had well earned, as they had not been paid for all their years of forced labour. Well, of all the things that have ruined men in the world, ruined them body and soul, there are few that have done it so effectually as silver and gold. You wouldn't think it, but it is a fact. Some few weeks ago I was shown at Pompeii, the place in South Italy which was destroyed some 1,800 years ago by a frightful eruption of Vesuvius, the skeleton of a man who was said to have met his death in this way. He is believed to have been a slave. When everybody fled during that awful time he seems to have turned back, or else he had lagged behind in order to possess himself of some of the precious things which the rest had abandoned in their flight. He paid bitterly for yielding to avarice at that dread moment. The stream of falling ashes overtook him while he was dragging his treasures along, and there his remains were found centuries afterwards and by his side the gold ornaments for which he had paid with his life. That is rather a gruesome illustration of the manner in which an uncontrollable passion for gold will not only make a man stumble, but may drag him down to the grave.

How different was it, says the text, with our fathers, at least during the early days of their deliverance. Though God brought them out with silver and gold, there was not one that stumbled. Prosperity had not injured them. Their self-control and self-discipline made them proof against the danger of great and sudden riches.

In the next place their discipline was of immense service to one another. How would it have been possible to move that large mass of people unless each man gave up some of his own wishes for the good of the rest, and they had resolved to be mutually kind and helpful to one another, the old and the strong helping the young and the weak, and the young and the feeble obeying those who were older and stronger. In that large gathering of the tribes, there must have been a great many people with different ideas and notions. But they kept them well under control—they were wise enough to see that each must surrender something, and even suffer some inconvenience, so that all might be saved.

Need I point out to you, dear children, that that is the only way in which you can do any good to others, and by which you will deserve that good may be done to you by others. You belong to a family, the happiness of which depends upon each member putting some measure of restraint upon himself. You belong to a race and a community, the peace and safety of which can only be maintained if each member is content to do or to forego for the good of all. Inside your house and outside your house some form of discipline always awaits you. But you are not to be pitied—rather you are to be congratulated. The person to be pitied is he who never gives up anything for the sake of others ; for surely his heart will harden, and what else can he expect than that other hearts will harden against him.

Do you know how travellers in rough and mountainous districts, like the Alps, manage to cross them in safety ? By a very simple contrivance. A strong cord is fastened to every member of the party ; as they move along each one feels himself safer for being united to his neighbour. A stumble or a fall cannot be entirely prevented, but they all feel sure that there is at least no risk of any one being lost. At the same time there is another gain. As every one knows that the safety of others besides himself is at stake, it makes him walk more warily. So that there is a double advantage—first that all are more careful, and next that all are more brave than they otherwise would be.

So is it with the family tie, and with the tie of a common race that binds us together. Surely it is something for you, dear children, to feel that you are not alone, that you have parents, brothers, sisters, other dear relatives, who care for you and would do all in their power to guard you from ill. It is something too to know that you belong to an ancient race, whom God has chosen and preserved through thousands of years for His own gracious purposes, and who would not willingly lose a single son or daughter of Israel. This might well fill you with a certain courage of heart and self-respect. But there is also the other side, and that is that you on your part should have a sense of responsibility in regard to all you do and say ; so that it becomes your duty to move about with caution, remembering that one cord binds us all together, and that if one Jew or Jewess stumbles and sins all the rest feel the shock, the shame of it. Let me hope, therefore, that you will have the strength and the uprightness of heart to resolve that, so far as you are concerned, your family and your fellow Jews alike shall be able to say there was no one that stumbled among your tribes.

Once more I would ask you to remember that if you would serve your God faithfully it is by this same method of discipline alone that you can do so. The life of a good Jew is one long, though very varied discipline— discipline in working and resting, in eating and drinking, in thinking and praying. It is not enough that he

S.C.   I doesn't fall; he must be ever on watch and guard that he doesn't stumble. The religion to which you belong is not an easy-going one. People have from time to time tried to make it so; but they have not succeeded, for by the time they have made it easy going enough it is easily gone.

Now, of all your duties to God, the first and most important is—to obey! The prophet Samuel said to King Saul: "To obey is better than sacrifice." This has many meanings, but one meaning is the following. If you have read Scott's *Talisman* you will remember how Sir Kenneth leaves his post for a moment to save some one whom he thinks is in danger. He leaves his post to fight for some one he thinks in distress, to make a sacrifice. Yet his doing so caused a good deal of trouble; there really was no one in distress, it was a trick to get him away from his post. He was a sentinel, and ought to have remembered that his first duty was to watch at his post. It is better and holier to do one's duty and obey orders than to worry about other things to do and disobey orders. If you skip over your duty to get to something else, you will almost certainly stumble and fall in your hurry. Take this, then, to heart. To serve God demands discipline, it means giving up what you *would* for what you *should*. May you all be filled with this desire to obey and to serve, and as you strive to do your duty in life may there be among you no one that stumbles!

TIME

(*New West End Synagogue,*
1895.)

PSALM XC. 12 : " So teach us to number our days that we
may get us a heart of wisdom."

MY DEAR CHILDREN.—There is a boy of my acquaintance
who has a shocking memory for dates. Ask him any
well-known date in the history of the Jews or in the
history of England, and he is certain to make a mistake
in the answer. There is only one date he can recollect.
What do you think it is ? It is the date of his own
birthday.

And not only does he not forget that himself, he takes
good care nobody else shall forget it. For weeks before
that important day comes round, he will be reminding
his friends and relations that on such and such a day of
such and such a month, he will be so old. Evidently
that boy has learned to number his days and years.
Whether he has learned so to number them as to get
him a heart of wisdom, I would not like to say, lest, perchance, he should be among those who are assembled
here this morning.

But, dear children, the mere numbering of our days,
if it stirs no other thoughts within us than those that
have occupied the mind of the boy I was speaking about,
if it does not help in some way to get us a heart of

wisdom, is not of much use. It is like knowing the names of a lot of books without knowing what is in them. You see God gives us but a limited number of days and years, even to the most favoured among us, seventy or eighty years, says the Psalmist, and when you consider it, it does seem a foolish thing to fritter away any portion of your life-time, even the small fraction which belongs to your childhood, because, when once gone, there is no power in the world that can bring it back. Business people say, "Time is money"; but, of course, time is much more than money, because men sometimes lose money and they find it again or make more, but the year or the day or the hour lost, no effort or fortune can ever restore.

Now, it is especially in the spring-time of life that we do well to count our days. I don't for a moment say that we shall be excused if we are negligent about them at any other period. But this I do say, that we can least afford to waste that part of life when our minds and hearts are young, and everything we sow in them is likely to take root and flourish. Have you ever heard of the unfortunate nobleman of whom it was said that he used to lose half an hour every morning of his life and spent the rest of the day in looking for it? Even more to be pitied are the people who have lost or wasted the morning of their life, and have to struggle during the rest of their existence to make up for it.

How wisely has our Holy Faith tried to guard us against such an error! You remember, I suppose, in connexion with our festival of Passover, that there is a Divine command that from the morrow after the commencement of the festival until the next following holy day of Pentecost, every day has to be counted to the number of forty-nine days, making seven weeks. This happens just in the spring season. Then it is that the reviving year, with the returning sunshine, causes people to be most light-hearted; but then also it is that their time is most precious, and lest they should let this period slip by without taking good note of it and getting all the good out of it which it is able to yield, they are bidden to number each day, as it comes, and keep a correct record of it.

So is it with you, dear boys and girls; it is just at the time when you are tempted to give hardly any serious thought to the fleeting years because they are so much pleasanter than any other, that it is well for you to count not only your years but even your days, because they are so much fuller of opportunities of good work than any other.

If I were to ask any of you: How many years have you lived? you would probably say, ten years, twelve years, or some other number, according to your age last birthday. Would you be surprised to hear that, if you carefully look into it, you have done nothing of the sort, that you are not nearly so old as your answer would lead one to imagine? Let me explain the thing. When you go to bed at night, and sleep soundly all the night through, as I hope you do, and wake up in the morning, and you try to think back, what is it your memory catches on to! Why, the last thing done or said before you fell asleep. Of all the hours you spent in sleep you don't recollect anything; during that time, for aught you know of it, you might as well not have been living at all. It is a slice cut clean out of your life. Isn't it? Again, of all the time when you were infants, you remember nothing. Which of you can remember the least thing of what happened before you were four years old ? Well then, if I take a boy of twelve, I might say to him, my young friend, you have to take off right away nearly four years, the time during which you were an infant, the years that are a blank to you. That leaves you eight years. But from the time you were five years old, you have spent nearly twelve of every twenty-four hours in sleep ; that means you have got to deduct nearly four years more ; and there remains, therefore, not much more than four years, during which you have been conscious, that is, awake and aware of things—and that is about as long as you have really lived. Of course, what is true of a boy or girl of twelve is true, with proper changes, of children who are older or younger, and, if you think of it carefully, ought to take the conceit out of them, if there is any in them, on the score of age.

Also there is another thing to bear in mind if you want to number your days wisely. There are people who in the same space of time live longer, or, at least live more than others. They get so much more thought and work into a day. They fix their attention on what they are doing, and do it in half or quarter the time the idler or the loafer takes over it. The result is they have more time left for other things, and thus seem to actually live longer. I have known boys and girls to be hours over a lesson, which they might have finished in as many minutes. They have foolishly persuaded themselves that the doing of one's duty has only to be measured by the clock. They gave their hours to a task, but not their thoughts. Time spent like that is also clean out of their lives. It is no use making the mill go round when there is no corn in it. And

To give your time and not your mind
Is like turning a mill with nothing to grind.

Think over these things carefully, and they will help you to find out how long you have truly lived, to count your days so that you will get a heart of wisdom.

Now it is a strange thing that though, as I have tried to show you, all children are younger than their years, some of them fancy themselves to be much older than, even by the general way of reckoning time, they can boast to be. At least I think they must so fancy themselves, to judge by the airs they put on, and the manner in which they treat people older than themselves. Respect to the aged is one of the best signs in the young. If when young you are respectful, then when you are old you will probably be respectable, that is a person others can respect. "Rise up before the grey-head," says the Scripture. Yet I have seen children forget to treat even their mothers and fathers with the respect due to their age. It is a dreadful thing to hear a child contradict his mother, argue with her, and even refuse to believe that his mother is really and truly the wiser and cleverer of the two. I am sure such children have made a mistake in their counting. They really seem to think that their parents are younger than their own children!

There is a beautiful Eastern fable to the following effect. A gourd wound itself round a lofty palm, and in a few weeks climbed almost to the very top. "How old mayest thou be?" said the new-comer, the gourd, to the palm. "About a hundred years," was the answer. "A hundred years, and no taller! Why, only look, I have grown as tall as you in fewer days than you can count years!" "I know that well," said the palm, "every summer of my life a gourd has climbed up round

me, as proud as thou art, and as short-lived as thou
wilt be." And, dear children, that is perhaps one of
the reasons why the righteous man in the Psalms is
compared to a palm-tree—" the righteous shall flourish
like the palm-tree." Good people take a long time
growing. I hope that you will not be like the silly
gourd. I hope that you will rather grow up like the palm-
tree, that God will give you long lives to become good
and wise. Only you must number your days, number
them in such a way that you may get yourselves a heart
of wisdom.

First count your days in a spirit of thankfulness.
You have not lived long, that is true ; but how your
life has been crowded with blessings from the instant
when loving arms first enfolded you unto this very hour !
Food, shelter, clothing, companionship, education,
amusement, recreation—all these have been yours
through the human agents whom a loving God employs
for your sakes while His unsleeping Providence has been
keeping constant watch and ward over you, so that,
though it might be easy to tell the number of your days,
it would puzzle the best arithmetician among you to
tell the number of your blessings.

Next count your days in a spirit of thoughtfulness.
Look about you and think well over it whether, among
all those with whom you associate, those of your own
years, or older or younger than you, whether there are
none to whom you can be of use, none whose troubles
you can lessen, whose happiness you can increase. Do
not say, I am too young to be of service to anybody ;
service must be rendered to me. Children sometimes
ask, When shall I be responsible for my actions ? Is
it not when I am thirteen years of age ?—No, my young

friend, you are responsible for all you do, for all you leave undone, for the use of every instant of your time from the moment that you have the sense to think "When shall I be responsible?"

Count your days in a spirit of trustfulness. Let what God has done for you hitherto, and what He is doing for you now, lead you to trust Him for the future. For you, with God's blessing, the greater part of life is yet to come. The chances of doing a vast amount of good are much greater for you than for us who have left our childhood behind us.

Old people are sometimes spoken of as being "rich in days." But how can a person be properly called rich who has spent nearly all his money? It is those who have not yet spent it who are really rich. And you are the truly rich in days, because you have not nearly exhausted yours; you have only just begun to spend them. May more and more be granted to you, dear children, out of the treasure house of the eternal God, and may you have the grace to make a right use of them! May you grow in days and years, in health and strength, in knowledge and in goodness, in wisdom and in that which is the beginning and ought to be the end and aim of all wisdom—the fear of God!

LITTLE HEROES

(Great Synagogue, Chanuka,
December 8, 1901.)

HERE are some words, dear children, which I will read out of the oldest book that tells us the story of Chanuka.

1 Macc. ii. 64. "And ye, my children, be valiant, and show yourselves men in behalf of the Law; for therein shall ye obtain glory."

That was what the old priest Mattathias said to his sons, when he felt that he would not be able to fight much more, for he was not going to live much longer, and when he called his children around him, to give them a father's last words of loving advice. He it was who stirred the people up not to submit to the unjust and cruel power of Antiochus and the Syrians; he it was who fired the Jews with a passionate love for the law of God and for their holy faith, and when all was dark and sad for them, and the Temple had fallen into the hand of the enemy and had been shamefully defiled, still never lost hope and would not let his people lose hope. "Therefore ye, my children, be valiant." And with these words, and a blessing on his lips, he died.

And his children were indeed valiant, and so were the people; they did marvels of bravery, old and young, women and children; the few against the many, those that were weak in body and in weapons against those that seemed so strong in both, until at last the Temple was retaken by Judas the Maccabee and the place made holy again, and the lights were kindled in the golden lamp, as you have just been reminded, and the Jews could sing, just as we now sing to-day, praises of joy to the God in whose cause they had fought, and who had been their salvation.

Now, you must not think of those days of danger and struggle as something altogether gloomy and sad. On the contrary, those must have been glorious times, dear children, despite all the trouble they brought with them, those times which this festival of lights is intended to recall. A little nation, consisting mainly of peaceful tillers of the soil and rearers of cattle, were suddenly converted into a nation of soldiers, resolved to fight to the death for hearth and home, for their faith and their God ; and this handful of men, without resources, without training or experience in the art of war, lived to become the conquerors of mighty armies and great and skilful generals, to clear the land of the abomination of the heathen, and to establish the pure worship of the true God in the place He had chosen.

Yes, that must have been a glorious time, because it produced not only great heroes, but little heroes also. And by " little heroes " I mean not big people who did little deeds of bravery, but little people who did great ones.

Perhaps the most stirring story that has come down to us from those days is the account of the mother and her seven children whom King Antiochus tried to force to violate the law of their God. Tormented with whips and scourges, they remained immoveable. Then the tyrant, to conquer the stubborn will of the others, selected the eldest of the seven, and with every refinement of torture burnt him to death in the sight of his brothers and his mother. In vain : the resolution of the onlookers remained unshaken. The second was taken, and in his turn subjected to unutterable tortures. He was asked to belie his faith, or he should " be punished through every member of his body " ; but his only answer was a bold and defiant " No." The same fate befel them one after the other. Death had no terrors for them. " It is good," they said, " to be put to death by men, and to look for hope from God to be raised up again by Him." Their mother exhorted them, even while it wrung her heart, to remain steadfast and to die bravely, " because the Creator of the world would of His own mercy give them breath and life again, as they now regarded not themselves for His law's sake.

And when it came to the turn of the youngest, the King, finding his wicked will still thwarted, strove to persuade the child by promises of riches and royal favour to turn from the law of God. It was all to no purpose. Encouraged by his mother, now resigned to offer up her child upon God's altar, he rejected the King's offer, and turning to the executioners exclaimed, " Whom wait ye for ? I will not obey the King's commandment ; but I will obey the commandment of the law that was given unto our fathers by Moses." A fearful end awaited him also, and the mother, unable any longer to bear up under the weight of her sorrows, laid down her life, and joined her children " where the wicked cease from troubling and the weary are at rest."

Now I am quite sure you all love those great and noble heroes. I never came across a boy or girl who did not like to hear a story of a really brave person. That is a good sign—it shows that God has put the love of goodness and of courage into your hearts. But God is not satisfied with that, He wants us to do something. This is to take that love of courage which God has put into your hearts and to put it into your lives. It is well to love courage in others, but it is better to show it in ourselves. And that is the reason why all those fine stories have been written down about the brave men and women and boys and girls who saved the faith in the terrible days of Antiochus. First, to make us honour the brave, and so to stir us up and urge us on to copy them.

But how can one account for this heroic courage shown by our fathers and mothers in those times ? There is one very simple explanation : they feared God ; they then felt that no evil could befall them, because they didn't think death an evil. They said : No harm can happen to us if God is on our side. Let us obey His will, and we can face our enemies with courage. We fear God and therefore fear not man. One of the bravest men this country ever produced was a man named John Lawrence—who became Viceroy of India, and was made Lord Lawrence. He lived at the time of the Indian Mutiny, and it is said that it was chiefly through his skill and courage that India was saved to England, so much so that he came to be called the Saviour of India. Well, he was a man who did not know what to be afraid meant, though his life was for many years in scenes of constant danger : but he was also a very religious and a God-fearing man. And when he died and they buried him in Westminster Abbey, they put these words upon his tomb—you may see the words yourselves if you go to Westminster Abbey,—" He feared man so little because he feared God so much."

I look about me in this vast assemblage, and I would fain believe I see before me a great number of little heroes—of little people who have in them the true heroic stuff. Do not imagine that brave and noble deeds require to be performed on a big stage, or before a whole world of observers, and amidst loud trumpetings and noisy advertisement. There are heroes of the quiet, noiseless sort, dear to God and of much blessing to their fellows, without whom the world would indeed be much poorer than it is. Let me point out to you some of those who are enrolled among the band of heroes.

The child who is brought up in poverty and want, amidst a constant and terrible struggle for life, and who yet keeps free from the least taint of dishonesty or deception or falsehood, loathing it with heart and soul, and proves that an upright, self-respecting spirit can have its home quite as much in a crowded miserable tenement lodging as in a splendid palace—that child belongs to the band of heroes. The boy who, having some honourable career in view, allows nothing to turn him from his purpose, who day in day out pursues his aim with an unfaltering will, who listens not to the voice of the tempter, charm he ever so wisely, who is content to "scorn delights and live laborious days," and to *wait* for his reward as well as to work for it and *earn* it—he is of the true order of heroes. The girl who takes her share in the burdens of a humble household, who, when sickness and sorrow have broken down the props and supports of her home, turns her hands to whatever she can in honour find to do, who gives up her own pleasures that others may be made happier, or at least may be spared further misery—she is a heroine.

The youth and the maiden who are mindful in all things, in the hour of work and in the hour of play, of their good name, who remember that they live for something higher than to eat and drink and be amused, who stoutly refuse to follow the multitude if the multitude run to do evil, who in an age when it is so hard a thing to be a Jew feel it would be harder still not to be one —they, and such as they, are members, all unconsciously to themselves perhaps, of the noble band of heroes.

You must never be afraid of being Jews, or of being known as being Jews. The only thing you need be afraid of is being bad Jews. The other day I heard a story at one of the great hospitals. Two little girls came in together to see two sick relations who were in one of the wards. A nurse went up to them, and said to the one, " What is your name ? " " Mary." " And what Church do you belong to ? " " Church of England." " Well," she said, "you may thank God for that." And then she saw the other who was standing by. " What is your name." "Sarah." "Oh," she said, "you are a Jewess." "Yes," answered the little girl, " and I thank God for that." It wasn't said saucily, you know, but nicely and quite respectfully, but firmly as if she felt that it would be mean to deny it, that it was something to be indeed proud of and grateful to God for. And the nurse wasn't at all angry. She was a heroine herself ; most nurses are brave and good as well as kind. And being brave herself, she loved this brave little girl, and said to her : " Yes, thank God for it, and show your thanks by being true to it."

Now, though the list I gave you just now—of the ways in which you can be heroes—is a long one, the list might be greatly enlarged. One form there is in which every one of you will at some time or other be called upon to show courage and heroism, and that is in having to say, when occasion demands, a very simple word very distinctly and very decisively — the word, " No."

Observe one important matter in that touching story of the mother and her seven sons. When the tyrant had made his demand of these faithful followers of the law of God, there does not seem to have been any long consideration on their part. They did not say to the King, Well life is very dear to us ; we will think over it for a day or two, and let you know. They answered at once and without hesitation, each one as his turn came, and with the same firmness, No ! God's will is more to us than yours. We will obey Him and not you.

How much wretchedness and ruin has been brought into the homes and hearts of men and women, and of boys and girls, because they could not say that word, or because they said it in a half-hearted way, so that it sounded very much like " yes," and in the end was really turned into " yes." Learn early to guard yourselves against evil companionship and evil example, and when the temptation comes to you, as come it will, to sin against God's law, be it in matters of truthfulness, or of honesty, or of purity, or of love and gentleness— the moment your conscience whispers " no," let your lips take up the message and proclaim aloud, clearly as with trumpet notes, " No ! "

Do these things seem to you but mild and weakly forms of heroism ? They are just such as God expects of you, because they are within the range of your powers. They are small beginnings, but not to be despised on that account; small beginnings, but full of promise of greater results.

Let me tell you of a curious and interesting circumstance. Across the Niagara river, a little below the celebrated falls of Niagara, the most stupendous cataract in the world, there runs a great suspension bridge. It is formed of a single span, 821 feet in length, with no support underneath, the whole upheld by four huge iron cables, each cable, if you cut it through, having an area of about sixty square inches. Now how do you think they got such a cable over the rushing river ? This is what they did. They took a kite, and when the wind was favourable they flew the kite over to the other shore. The people on the opposite side secured the toy with its string, and now they had a thin insignificant thread uniting the two banks. To that string they attached a stouter one, then a cord, then a stronger one still, then a rope, then a cable powerful enough to hold the iron cable, which was thus at length drawn across, and now sustains a bridge twenty-five feet broad, over which heavily laden trains pass to and fro in safety. That is what comes from small beginnings. And so every act of youthful courage, and fortitude, and heroism, small as it may seem, is but the beginning that makes greater acts possible in after life. Little by little the chain is lengthened, strengthened and enlarged, until the whole of your lives shall be spanned by a glorious bridge of noble and heroic deeds.

Do not then underrate what you can do, as boys and girls, because it appears to you little in comparison with what you have heard of the world's renowned heroes and heroines. God asks of us exactly what we *can* do. We may leave the rest to Him. And mar-

vellously He often helps us. You have all heard the
Chanuka legend, how when the Maccabees had recovered the Temple, and wished to rededicate it, to restore
the service as aforetime, and to kindle the perpetual
light of the candelabrum, they could find but a single
flask of consecrated oil that could be used for that
purpose. Those brave soldiers and pious priests might,
had they so chosen, have neglected this duty altogether.
They might have said, Of what use is it to light the
sacred lamp at all ? the light can but last for a day,
and then must follow many days during which the
house of God will be in darkness for lack of holy oil.
But they did not reason thus ; they said, Thus much
it is in our power to do : let us not neglect it because
it is not more.

Ah, dear children, if we waited until we could render
our whole debt to God, we should have to wait for ever.
Happily for us, God asks not of us according to *His*
measure, but according to *our* measure. If we never
prayed to Him until we could pray in a manner worthy
of Him, we should never be able to commence. If we
would thank Him as He deserves, our whole life would
have to flow in ceaseless praise. But God is gracious,
not only in what He gives us, but in what He asks and
in what He accepts from us, and when we do but kindle
the pure light of devotion in our hearts, the good God
who looks to the intentions more than to the actual
achievements of men smiles lovingly and approvingly
upon our efforts, aids us in our weakness, supplies our
deficiencies, until the soul of man becomes a veritable
lamp of God.

And now, dear children, all stand up and repeat with
me this prayer.

Almighty God! we thank Thee for all Thy love and kindness to us. We thank Thee that Thou didst raise up in times past men and women true, and brave, and godly, who loved Thy holy Word, and guarded it with their lives, and whose deeds we this day recall to Thy glory, to their honour, and as an example to ourselves. Help us, O Lord! to be also strong and of good courage, to do Thy will at all times, in great things and in small, before the eyes of others or hidden from them, whether the world be with us or against us. May we have the courage to fear no one but Thee, to fear to displease Thee, our heavenly Father, by aught that is mean, or unclean, or untrue, or unholy.

We pray to Thee on behalf of our brethren of the house of Israel. Be now their guardian still. We pray to Thee on behalf of this our dear country, where every right and liberty is ours, and of our beloved King and all his royal house. We ask Thy blessing on all men, of all races and creeds; for have we not all one Father; hath not one God created us? Soon may they learn to seek their highest glory in Thee, so that all Thy children may with one heart know Thee and serve Thee for ever!

SELF-CONTROL

(*An undelivered sermon.*)

EXODUS xiv. 13, 14 : " And Moses said unto the people, Fear ye not, stand still, and see the salvation of the Lord, which He will work for you to-day : for the Egyptians whom ye have seen to-day, ye shall see them again no more for ever. The Lord shall fight for you, and ye shall hold your peace."

THERE is an old story in the books of the old Jewish Rabbis or teachers, which tells us that the Israelites when they got to the Red Sea after their escape from Egypt were very excited. Now Israelites always were and always are rather excitable. But they were especially excitable on that occasion. They were all right when everything went well and smoothly; but when things were not well and smooth, and the Egyptians were hurrying up behind them and the sea was in front of them, they grew so excited that Moses had his hands full.

And they all wanted to do different things ; they had not yet learned to trust God and Moses in time of danger ; and so they cried out all at once, giving one another different advice and wanting to do different things. Four classes especially were among them. Some said, Let us throw ourselves into the sea ; others said, The best thing we can do is go back to Egypt ; others said, Let us go to meet the Egyptians and fight them ; and others, Let us shout against them and see what will happen. And it is said that it is to these different kinds of people who wanted to do what God didn't want them to do, Moses spoke in the words I just read to you. To those who said, Let us drown ourselves in the sea, Moses said, " Fear not, but stand firm and see the salvation of the Lord." To those who wanted to get out of their trouble by going back to live in Egypt once more as slaves, Moses said, No, no, as you have seen the Egyptians to-day you shall never see them again. To those who wanted to give battle to the Egyptians he said, Restrain yourselves, " the Lord will fight for you." And those who thought that shouting would be useful were told—You be quiet. Then when he had got them all in order, Moses did what they had not thought of, and appealed to God Himself, and from Him came the command, Speak to the children of Israel that they journey forward.

Now what is the lesson you can take away with you from these words ? It is the lesson of self-control, self-discipline. Sometimes it is stand firm, sometimes it is journey forward ; and very often it is just when we want to move that we have to stand, and just when we want to stay that we have to move forward. But we have all got to learn this lesson of self-discipline and self-control, whether we are young or whether we are old—only it is easier to learn it when we are young than when we are old, and if it is put off too long it may be too late to learn it at all.

Now if you think of it you will remember that all the commands of our Religion are of two kinds—thou shalt not, or thou shalt : all the duties of life are like these. Either you mustn't or you must. Children sometimes think it hard that there are so many you mustn'ts and you musts in their life, and they would like to do—well, just as they like ; and there are even many clever and well-disposed grown-up people who have tried all sorts of experiments in what is called education to make things easy and pleasant for the children—so that they may be trained without knowing it, but they have never found a way of sparing them the musts and the mustn'ts, at least not in those who shall grow up true men and women. We have all got to learn for ourselves—and no one can learn it for us, and no one can save us from it—to control our desires, to control our tempers, to control our tongues, to control our actions.

It is so in little things and in great things. For instance, night comes on, and a child thinks, How annoying it is that I must go and lay me down to rest in my bed just when I want to be like others and sit up late ; but those who know what is best say, No, no, you musn't ; you cannot have your own way. And then the morning comes, and perhaps you don't want to get up, and like the sluggard in the Book of Proverbs you say, A little more sleep, a little more slumber, a little more folding of the hands in sleep ; but the duties of the day have to be done, and you are told, Rise you must.

And in other ways, too, you have to learn to control your desires. Some boys and girls, for instance, are rather greedy ; or rather they do not know how to control themselves when they have nice things to eat placed before them. I once knew a little boy who caught a live mole. It is not easy, because moles do not often come out when people are about. But he caught it, and brought it home. He got a large, deep earthenware bowl, filled it with mould and put the mole in. In a second the mole had vanished ; it burrowed its way down and hid itself. Well, the boy collected masses of earthworms for the mole to eat, and when the boy went to bed, he left a great lot of the worms in the bowl so that the mole should have a little snack when it felt disposed. Next morning the boy came down to look at the mole, but he found it—dead. It had eaten up *all* the food and had simply gorged itself to death. The mole was a victim to lack of self-control.

That was a sad instance, and surely none of my young hearers need to have the moral of it explained for *their* benefit. I hope that you can control yourselves better than that. For a large part of your education is simply a long lesson in controlling your desires. You must also control your bodies. Some children have a dreadful habit of getting themselves in the way. They cannot keep their legs and hands out of trouble, and often hurt themselves simply because they are clumsy. What is clumsiness but lack of control ? If a boy is bowling overarm, and bowls wide—as I have often seen boys do—it is because he has not yet learned to control his arm. And the result is that he not only misses the wicket which he ought to hit, but he hits things he ought to miss. If you do not control yourself, others suffer. So, too, if a girl is playing hockey, and gets her stick too high, she very likely strikes another player. She is quite a nuisance to other players until she can control herself. But I need not say any more about this.

Speaking of games reminds me of another thing you have to control—your tempers. It is shocking to play with a bad-tempered child, who only keeps amiable while all goes well. If he wins, such a boy may be pleasant enough in a surly sort of way ; but if he loses he is disagreeable and sulks. Some children are always quarrelling. " I won't play "—that is what they are continually saying. They won't play the game the others want, they won't field because they would rather bat, they won't do this and won't do that, and all because they cannot control their temper. They make every one miserable, and they make themselves miserable. The only happy child is the child that can control its temper. And the worst of it is that children who cannot control their tempers mostly cannot control their tongues. They say rude things, bitter things, and unkind things. And sometimes—even untrue things. " I *wasn't* out "—such a boy will say when he really *was* out. Dear me, when you come to think of it, what an enormous deal depends on self-control. The reason why, for instance, it is good for boys to learn boxing—apart from its training to them defend themselves—is just this : it teaches them not to lose their temper.

Bravery is only another name for self-control. Let me tell you this. The bravest people are not those who are never afraid. If you are never afraid, it may merely be that you are too ignorant to realize the danger. But if you know that a thing is dangerous, and if you really feel that you ought to do it, then you are brave because you control your fears, not because you have no fears. Little Spartan boys were brought up to bear anything, no matter how it hurt, rather than give in or cry. I have read somewhere of a little girl in Holland. She lived in a very flat part where the water is kept out by dykes. One evening she was passing by a dyke and saw the water trickling through. She knew that if the water was not at once stopped there would be a great risk that the whole village would be flooded, and that her parents and little brothers and sisters and many others would be drowned. So she put her finger in the hole, and it just fitted. She kept it there for hours and hours ; the pain was dreadful, for her finger got numbed and swollen. At last her father, who had been everywhere looking for her, found her at the dyke. They had to cut a hole in the dyke to get her finger out, and they took her home where she lay ill for weeks. But she had saved the village, and all by her wonderful self-control. For I need hardly tell you that they mended the dyke very securely.

I will give you another instance, from Jewish history. When Judas Maccabeus was fighting the Syrians, the enemy tried to trap him by a night surprise. They sent a detachment of 5,000 men over the hills after him, to get behind him and his small army, while they left their main body in the camp in the plain. But Judas crept round and attacked the camp while the detachment was searching for him. He won the victory, and his men wanted to stop in the Syrian camp and enjoy themselves and rest. " No ! " said Judas, " remember the 5,000 men ! We have another fight before us ! We cannot rest yet." And so they won the second fight too. Was not that splendid self-control ? *That* is the spirit by which we conquer the dangers and difficulties of life. Each victory we win strengthens us for another victory, if we only learn how to govern ourselves.

You have all lately read of Mount Vesuvius, the volcano near Naples in Southern Italy, how active it has been, throwing out for many days, with terrible explosions, vast masses of glowing ashes and stones and lava, which have made ruin of many fair villages and fertile lands and have caused the death of hundreds of people. More than 1,800 years ago, in the year 79 of the Christian Era, there was an awful eruption of that same volcano much worse than the one of the last week or two. It completely destroyed two great cities that had grown up at its base, Pompeii and Herculaneum, with many of its unfortunate inhabitants. Besides other matter it cast out huge masses of ashes, cinders and thin volcanic dust, and these mixed with steam formed a kind of pasty mud which overwhelmed these cities and their inhabitants, and filled up every hollow space, rising some twelve to twenty-four feet above the highest buildings. In course of time the clay thus formed hardened, and has been the means of preserving to a great extent all that it had overwhelmed, so that when in modern times people began to dig out the place they found things just as they were when destruction overtook the cities so many hundreds of years ago. The bodies of the unfortunate people, who mostly perished from poisonous fumes, were of course shrunken away, but their forms were left in the hardened clay as in a mould, and by pouring liquid plaster into those open spaces and letting it dry, it has been possible to get almost exact copies of some of those unhappy folk, just where and how they died. There, for instance, is a slave who, thinking in the confusion he could carry off some of his master's property and make it his own, had got precious vessels in his grasp ; then there is a mother carrying off, what do you think—what was most precious to her, her little babe, and trying to cover and protect it with her own body. But the reason why I have referred to this event is because among others there is said to have been found the body of a Roman soldier. He was a sentinel mounting guard, standing with a spear in his hand, and it looks as if having been put there on duty he would not desert his post. The rain of ashes and mud fell and mounted higher and higher until at last it engulfed him. There was self-control and discipline if you like! The poor brave fellow died—we must all die—and since we must all die, is it possible for a man to die more nobly than at his post of duty?

A Rabbi asked: " Who is really a strong man? " And he answered: " He who can control his disposition." That, dear children, is the true heroism. More mighty is he who governs himself than he who captures a fortress. May you all become heroes in this sense; may you learn how to control yourselves; how to place duty before pleasure; how to be unselfish; how, in short, to give up your own desires so as to do the desire of your Father in heaven! As at the Red Sea, so now and always, He will be by your side to help you and to fight for you, if only you will show yourselves worthy of His aid.

WORKERS, WISE AND WILLING

A Sermon delivered before the Apprentices of the Jewish Board of Guardians, in the Great Synagogue,

(On Sabbath Afternoon, March 14th, 1903.)

EXODUS xxxv. 10: " And every wise hearted among you shall come and make all that the Lord hath commanded."

AND then follows a long list of all that was to be made, objects of the most various kinds required in the construction and for the Service of the Tabernacle. And after that, an account of how the people, men and women, freely and with willing hearts gave not only of their substance, but of their time, their labour and their skill, and how finally the Sanctuary stood complete in all its parts, the whole, from the simplest portions to the most complex, the work of Israelitish hands. Who shall dare to doubt after that that Jews are fit for any work good and true, useful and beautiful ?

Now I want you to notice in the first place this. Who is it that is to come and make the various things here described ? " Every one that is *wise hearted* among you." Fools never make anything—except mischief. Fools never make things ; they only mar them. It is the wise-hearted that become real makers and workers, producers of something of use in the world. And see what honour is paid to the real worker. In Hebrew he is sometimes called a " Choshev," i.e. a thinker, a title which is earned by him who works not only with his

140

fingers but with his brains, and puts his soul into the labour of his hands.   Nay more.   It is said of the chief worker of that time that he was " filled with the spirit of God."   The artist workman is thus ranked with the prophet.   In different ways and in different degrees inspiration comes to them both.   Not upon Moses only but upon Bezaleel also the spirit of God rested.   His very name, say our sages, bespeaks the man.   Bezaleel means " In the Shadow of God," for the faithful worker lives, as it were, under the shadow of God—ever mindful whence he has derived his gifts, and whom he is to glorify by means of them, and more bent upon doing some noble work than eager for the earthly fame and profit thereof.

In the next place observe that it is said these wise-hearted people " *shall come and make* all that the Lord hath commanded."   They are not to be driven to it. They are to do it willingly or it will lose its value in God's eyes.   God loves a cheerful worker.   If men will do nothing except under compulsion, I do not see how theirs can be acceptable work ; I am sure it will never be first-class work.   The chief glory of the Tabernacle, humanly speaking, lay in this, that it was the product of a people who were both wise-hearted and willing-hearted. And then notice further the words " shall come and make *all that the Lord hath commanded.*"   The work was naturally of many sorts and of many degrees of impor-tance.   But it was all good and holy work, since God had commanded it all.   If all those capable of work had fas-tened upon the same thing ; if, for instance, they had said, we will have to do with nothing but gold and silver and precious stones, the tabernacle would not have been finished to this day.   You see then that all work which God has commanded is good and holy, but it needs, whatever it be, first wisdom and next willingness.

Now if you were to ask, " What is the first thing God wants us to make as we grow into men and women ? " I should say, He wants us to make a *living*. As to our parents when they quitted Paradise, so also to us, when we leave the Paradise of our childhood behind us, and have to begin the world for ourselves, the word of God comes, " In the sweat of thy brow thou shalt eat bread." That is, Thou shalt earn a living for thyself. Hard work though it may sometimes be, it is also holy work. But to make a proper living you too need wisdom of heart. You must *learn* some useful occupation before you can profitably follow it. There you are indeed fortunate. For you are one and all learning the greatest art, and at the same time the highest duty, the duty and the art of earning a livelihood for yourselves. I want you to consider for a moment the immense advantage many of you have over your parents or grandparents. In many cases they have come from countries where life was made very bitter to them. In those lands the Jew is hampered on every side. The schools are practically closed against him. Though the Jews, in certain parts, are as numerous as the Christians, or more numerous, they are allowed only one place in ten, or one in twenty, in the schools. If, in spite of all efforts to keep him down, a Jew manages to master a trade or a profession, the chances are that he will not be allowed to practise it. He may have plenty of brains ; he may have deft and skilful hands ; he may have the best desire in the world to lead a useful life—it all counts for nothing. Is it not enough to drive one desperate ? Now compare all this with what happens here. The schools are open

to all ; sometimes indeed, as you perhaps know, children
are made to enter them even against their will.   There
is no question of religion.   The technical schools, too, are
available for all alike.   Every occupation is open to you
for which you are fit.   All you have to do is to prove
yourselves fit.   That may take time and trouble ; and
it may cost money.   You have to give the time and
trouble ; and the Board provides the money, until
you are in a position to repay it.   Whenever you feel
a bit discontented with your lot, just think to yourselves,
my young brothers and sisters, what your state would
be if you were living in any of those countries from which
you, your parents or grandparents have happily got free.

We have heard a great deal of late about the unemployed.   It is one of the saddest things in the world
that there should be so many people wanting work and
yet unable to find it, and condemned in consequence to
suffer hunger and cold and the lack of the ordinary
necessaries of existence.   Some of them, no doubt,
are idlers, but most of them, I am sure, are not, and do
not want to be.   Only, if you look closely into the matter,
you will find it is mostly the unskilled workmen who
suffer when there is slackness in trade.   Very many of
those who go about the streets singing, " We've got no
work to do," speak the truth so far as it goes, but it
doesn't go far enough.   They ought to say, " We've got
no work to do, and if we had, we couldn't do it."   They
are not only unemployed, they are unemployable.
Make yourselves masters of some useful and honourable
trade, and you will be the very last who will have to
fear such a fate.   There is a fine saying in the Talmud :
" Seven years the famine lasted ; but it never came near
the door of a workman."

But, besides knowledge, willingness is needed to make a successful worker—willingness which shows itself by a desire for constant improvement, by punctuality, and regularity at your place of apprenticeship, by avoiding frivolous complaints, by endeavouring to live at peace with your fellow-workers, by striving to please your masters, and not having too great an opinion of yourselves. In the ancient tabernacle some parts of the work were naturally inferior to others. There must also have been a good deal of mess and litter made, which had to be swept up and cleared away. Yet all these operations were but the several parts of " the work of the sanctuary." There are people nowadays who think it a fine thing to show themselves very sensitive about the work they are wanted to do. All sorts of things are derogatory to them. I have heard of an apprentice who took it as an insult to be asked to sweep the shop he worked in and had helped to make unclean. Well, an apprentice who starts with too high a sense of his importance will probably end by convincing everybody of his insignificance. It is related of a benevolent lady, one of the noblest among her people, that one day, visiting among her less fortunate sisters, she came to the house of one who had fallen into poverty from comparative comfort. She found her sitting in a room the windows of which had evidently not been cleaned for a long time. " What makes my life so sad," said the unfortunate woman, " is the knowledge that I have seen brighter days." " That may be," replied the lady, " but you will never see brighter days again if you don't clean your windows and let sunlight in." " What ! clean windows ! I couldn't do it. It is not what I have been accustomed to." " Couldn't you do it ? Well, let me try." And the Baroness Lionel de Rothschild got a cloth, mounted a chair, used a quantity of elbow grease, and made quite a tidy job of it.

Of course, if you object to every kind of rough work, your progress is likely to be very slow. There are plenty of ambitious people in the world who would really like to excel in the mastery of all sorts of handicrafts, but who will not bend themselves to the hard work by which alone such mastery can be attained. Into the office of a great engineering firm there once stepped a young gentleman, dressed in the height of fashion, with spotless kid gloves on his hands. He wished to consult the head of the firm, a man who, by his own industry and character, had risen from the position of a common workman to be head of a world-famed house. " I wish to be an engineer," said the visitor, " how am I to set about it ? " " The first thing you must do," answered the other, " is to take your gloves off." " And then ? " asked the young gentleman, a little nettled. " Oh, the next thing is, take your coat off."—There is a good deal of sense in that answer. Do you want to succeed in any career ? Then you must put all your strength, and skill and will into it. You mustn't object to rough it. You mustn't mind even dirtying your hands, providing you don't forget to wash them afterwards. You will never learn your trade in a frock coat and kid gloves. Nor will you do yourselves much good if you get the notion into your head that certain trades, the easy and well-paying ones, are fit for Jews, and that the others must be left for the Gentiles ; or that you ought to avoid certain trades because they are not clean enough for you. Depend upon it the trades to which the Board apprentices you are all of them clean trades. You need not be more jealous on that account than your friends at the Board. It is the way in which the worker conducts his trade or business that makes it clean or unclean. There is, indeed, a defilement that comes from indolence, from slovenliness, from dishonesty, from disregard of solemn obligations. From all that sort of uncleanness may you keep yourselves free, whatever the walk of life you may make your own. Apply yourselves steadfastly with wise and willing hearts to the calling you have chosen, and the blessing of the Lord will rest upon the work of your hands.

To the parents of our apprentices who are in this assemblage, I would also appeal. Do your part, my friends, in the good work of making your children good workers. Insist upon their attention to every point of duty. Love them by all means, but do not pamper them. " It is good for a man to bear the yoke in his youth." Bear it our children must, but it will become easier, and they will be spared much, if they have learnt to bear it in their youth. Have the thousands who have learnt no trade, have the " greeners " in the sweater's den such an easy time of it ? Don't be impatient if your children's progress is slow, nor in a hurry to cancel their indentures at the first difficulties. Do not be too ready to persuade yourselves that your children are too *schwach* (weak) for their work. That excuse has proved the ruin, both in body and in soul, of more than one capable young worker. Especially help your children by your influence and example to be, and to remain, good Jews. Happily the Board tries to secure in every instance that its apprentices shall have their Sabbaths and holy days free. But the Board cannot see to it that these oppor-tunities are rightly used. That is your duty. Help them above all to keep the honour of the Jewish name pure and unsullied. Never was there a time in this country when there was a stronger call upon every one of us, rich and poor alike, to combine all our efforts for this sacred purpose. And we shall succeed—if we give heed to the word of our great teacher : " Every wise-hearted among you shall come and make all that the Lord hath commanded."

THE STRENGTH OF LITTLE THINGS

(*New West End Synagogue,*
Passover, 1897.)

SONG OF SOLOMON ii. 15 : " Catch for us the foxes, the little foxes that spoil the vineyards ; for our vineyards are in blossom."

THE book from which these words are taken is a very wonderful little book, which you will perhaps understand better when you are older, although it is possible you will never understand it entirely, because the oldest and wisest men are not quite sure that they can make it all out. A great many big books have been written about that little book, so it must be hard to make out. But any one who reads it with a simple mind and heart, and without any help at all from clever people, can see that it is all about spring, and flowers, and trees, and gardens, and country life, and about Love— love tender and true, strong as death, and faithful through all trials. And because there was great love between God and His people, and God showed His greatest love for His people by bringing them out of Egypt that they should be His people, and He be their God, and because this happened just in the spring season, when nature is at its loveliest, especially in that part of the world where our fathers lived, therefore we are taught to read this book and think upon it at this very Festival of Passover.

148

In the midst of a scene of great charm and beauty some one is heard calling out, " Catch for us the foxes, the little foxes that spoil the vineyards ; for our vineyards are in blossom." The speaker and his friends are much concerned about the mischief these creatures do. The fox is said to be rather fond of grapes, and most certainly his cousin, the jackal, is, who is the animal usually meant by the Hebrew word translated " fox." You all remember the fable of the Fox and the Grapes, how he longed for them very much until he found he could not get at them, and then comforted himself by saying that no doubt they were sour and not worth having. In Palestine it would be easier to get at them, for the vines there grown trail rather low, and near the ground. Besides, the young foxes do special harm to the vineyards, for they rush about and overturn and ruin things both on account of the playfulness of youth and on account of the foxiness that is in them. A gentleman who has been to the Holy Land and looked about him a good deal while he was there, has told me that at the present time, just as in the time of the Bible, every well-cultivated field and vineyard has to be watched day and night against the visits of these pests, young and old. In the vineyard is a raised structure, a look-out, and there the watchers remain, taking it in turns and never leaving the place unguarded. Scarecrows do not seem to be of much use against these bold little robbers.

But there is another way in which it is possible for the fox to do damage to the vineyard. You know that the fox lives in a cave or burrow underground. In fact, the fox is said to be called *shūāl* in Hebrew from a root which has the sense of *hollowness*, because of the pit or underground hole where he dwells. This consists of one main and a number of side passages in which he takes refuge from his enemies and where it is not easy to follow him. There he and Mrs. Fox bring up their family, generally from five to eight little cubs at a time, and as they soon become very restless and romp about underground—though foxes usually prefer other animals to do the hard work of burrowing for them—they may cause injury to the tender vine-roots and consequently to the vines themselves. So you will understand the cry of the countrymen : " Catch for us the little foxes that spoil the vineyards ; for our vineyards are in blossom."

Now, dear children, I fancy some of you will say, What has all this to do with us ? There are no vineyards in Bayswater or in Kensington, or in Notting Hill, or Maida Vale. And if there were, there are no foxes to spoil them, young or old. Be not so sure. " The vineyard of the Lord of hosts is the House of Israel, and the men of Judah are His pleasant plant," says the prophet Isaiah. Nay more, each human heart is a vineyard—the younger, the more precious, because the blossom is on it ; and what injures it most, ruins the fruit when it ripens or prevents it ever properly ripening, is not always some big sin or terrible crime such as shocks the world, but the little failings, the little faults, the little sins to which we give a home in our own hearts, and which we do not think it worth while to dislodge.

Why, it does not require animals so large even as little foxes to destroy the vineyards. There is a little insect called the phylloxera, which was brought to Europe from America some thirty years ago. It is so small that between thirty and forty go to an inch. But for many years it threatened to ruin all the vines in France and Germany and other vine-growing countries. It multiplied at such a tremendous rate that unless some cure for it had been found, there would probably not be a healthy vine in existence to-day.

And so it may be with many of our little sins. We may think lightly of them ; we may look upon them as harmless ; we may consider them too small to notice ; but they are all the while doing us terrible injury, and evil indeed will it be for us if we only find them out when they have grown too large or too many to be suppressed by us. Little lapses from truth and honour, little indulgences in greed and selfishness, little yieldings to a feeling of spite and jealousy, little deeds and words of unkindness, little failures in dutifulness to mother and father, little acts of faithlessness to God—they all tell upon us. They grow stronger, while we grow weaker. Catch for us the little foxes that destroy the vineyards—especially when our vineyards are in blossom. If you want to tame and govern your faults, you must catch them young. You must master them when they are young, or they will master you when you are old.

Take, in particular, one kind of little fault only, the faults of temper. I mention that, because people generally feel, and there is no doubt something in it, that faults of temper do not amount to a great sin. Perhaps not, but they may easily become so. They may make our whole life and that of others, even our very nearest and dearest, gloomy and hard to bear. Would you not call that a sin ? If we let the brute passions become lord over that which is divine within us, and conquer all sense of justice and love, is not that a sin ?

That is the very sort of fault which you must catch and tame while you are young, or you will never do it.

We have been a good deal in the company of animals this morning, and so I may be permitted to refer to another beast whose acquaintance most of you will already have made—I mean the rhinoceros at the Zoo. I know some one who takes quite a friendly interest in that rhinoceros, though the rhinoceros does not return his kindly feelings. He was speaking the other day to the animal's keeper about him, and was told that never once since the rhinoceros' arrival had he been in a good temper. He is about forty-two years old, he has been twenty-two years in the Gardens, and has been in a bad temper all the time. Imagine twenty-two years of un-broken ill temper ! He must have had no early training, or it was thrown away upon him. But that is the difference between the young of the human species and a rhinoceros calf. Early training, and, above all, early self-training takes the place of iron bars for life.

It is a curious thing to notice how often people who are proof against great sins fall into little ones, with results almost as bad to their characters as if they had been guilty of the greatest. They would not, for instance, rob a man of his purse, but they do not mind if they take away his character. They would not defraud anybody, but they don't think it any harm to mislead others with words used in a double sense. They would not torture a fellow-man, for that would be cruel, but they con-stantly say sharp little things that wound others' feelings, not perhaps as though they were being hacked with swords but as if they were pierced with pin-pricks. They would not be guilty of blasphemy and defy God to His face, but they think it a small offence to laugh at sacred things, or to be wanting in respectful behaviour even in God's House. These things all mount up and go a long way to condemn those who practise them, to condemn them all the more severely because they are apt to think themselves so much better than other people.

On a certain dangerous coast, where many ships went up and down, a lighthouse was set up. It was built of the best material ; the best work was put into it ; it was furnished with the best instruments, and manned by the ablest keepers. One night, when it was more than usually dark, and when the light was most needed to guide passing mariners on their way, it refused to shine out. When the men examined it they found that the brilliant light had drawn to it such crowds of little insects as to cover and dim the glass. Neither waves nor wind nor storms could hurt the lighthouse ; but these myriad little creatures, each insignificant in itself, wellnigh rendered the whole lighthouse useless.

So also is it with human beings. Some of them may have the will and the strength to resist great temptations, but they yield to so many little ones as to darken and deface the brightness and beauty of their characters.

But now let me tell you another story of a different kind. Dear me ! It is, after all, about animals again !

In ancient ages the old Egyptians were marvellously pleased with their noble river, its flowing waters and its fertile banks. Upon these banks they settled themselves ; but before long there came up from the river those monstrous and voracious creatures called crocodiles, which damaged their fields and farms and preyed upon human lives, especially upon the young. In all sorts of ways the Egyptians tried to rid themselves of the terrible invaders : they reared temples, and called upon their god Osiris, but Osiris didn't hear them, or at least he didn't help them ; they armed themselves with swords and staves, but in the battle they often got the worst of it, so thick was the skin of the horrid creature ; they threw up dykes and mounds, but it was of little use. Only for a short time could they drive the crocodile back, for he returned and multiplied and fearfully ravaged their country. Then they gave all up as lost, and as they could not conquer him, they worshipped him ; they cried, " Great is the crocodile." Of their own accord they brought him fat victims and adored him as a god. One day there came among them a messenger sent from heaven, a good and wise priest, and he said to them, " God has heard your cries, follow me, and I will show you how you will be rid of the crocodile." So he led them along the side of the Nile, and pointed out to them, as they went, a little creature which they had not noticed before, and which afterwards came to be called Pharaoh's Mouse, or the Ichneumon, and he said : " See, this is your deliverer, this is the conqueror of the crocodile." The people supposed he was only mocking them, and as they didn't understand him or didn't agree with him, they, like ignorant people as they were, were very angry with him, and it is said even punished him very severely. What ! was it possible that such a little contemptible creature could do what they with all their ingenuity could not ? But the priest said, " Look " ; and lo ! while they were engaged in persecuting him, they saw the little Ichneumon, busy in scraping out of the sand the eggs of many crocodiles and destroying them. The people gazed in wonder and gladness. Soon the number of the tyrants and tormentors was lessened, because they were killed in the egg, and then it was the dwellers on the banks of the Nile came to understand how God often accomplishes very great ends by the most insignificant means.

Thus the power of little things is not only to be seen on the bad side, but fortunately also on the good side. As little sins injure and undermine the character, so little virtues strengthen and build it up. Most of us are probably not intended for great things, or for what the world considers great things. Let us make up our minds to that, and be contented. Yet, rightly understood, every good life is a great and glorious thing, and such a life is made up of attention to the little duties that are always and everywhere at hand. And even those who are called to the greatest positions in the world only reach them after they have been tried and found faithful in small and simple ones.

A few days ago there died a man, one of our own race, who in the course of a few years rose to be one of the most eminent lawyers, the leading barrister in what is known as the Admiralty Court, the court where law cases are tried connected with shipping and navigation. He early made up his mind to strive to become an authority on these subjects. It is upon our sea-going vessels and our seamen that, as you no doubt know, the strength, safety and prosperity of England depend. Now there are two ways of studying ships and sailors, and the laws and rules by which they are governed. One is by reading about them in books ; the other is by going to sea oneself, and learning everything about them from personal experience. The one way is perhaps the more pleasant, but the other is the only thorough way Well, Lionel Pyke actually went to sea and served for many months almost like any common sailor. No trifle about ships and sailors was too trifling for him to investigate and to study. The result was that nothing in his branch came amiss to him. He knew what he was talking about. People—judges and barristers and suitors—soon found it out, and his reward was to rise to the highest place in his profession, with the sure prospect, had it pleased God to spare him, of being elevated to be a judge in the very court where he was one of the most distinguished advocates.

But I say again, a good life is really the greatest thing on earth, and that is built up not by any one great effort, but " line upon line, observing precept upon precept, a little here, a little there." That is, for example, why we ought to rejoice that there has been formed in this and other districts a Children's Orphan Aid Society, which every one of you should join, and which, once having been joined, should never be forsaken by you. I mention this because the number of members does from time to time fall off. You put by your penny a week ; you send your thirteen pence at the end of every quarter to the Treasurer, and if that does not make you feel happy, why it ought to. For you are doing a great good to others by those small means : you are helping to support one of the poor children who have neither father nor mother, or are as badly off as if they had none. And not to them alone are you doing good, but to yourself also, and to yourself chiefly. You are gaining far more than you give. You are making a little sacrifice of your own every week, for I am supposing that you give the penny which is yours and are not charitable only with your parents' purse ; you are learning to do good regularly, punctually—a grand thing—and not by chance or by fits and starts, and you are fitting yourself for greater efforts by and by. Be sure, dear children, the little acts of mercy and loving-kindness you practise in your childhood will thrive and flourish until they become full-grown graces, and your life be crowned with the love of all good men and women, with the love of God Himself, the Father of all goodness.

GIVE THINE HEART

(New West End Synagogue, 1904.)

PROVERBS xxiii. 26 : " My son, give me thine heart."

WHAT is there, my dear children, that you may be sure
about if any one asked you, " Give me your heart ? "
You may be sure that the person who asks your love is
a person that cares about you, that loves you. For
he asks this of you *before* you have given what he asks.
In fact, if you had already given it, there would be no
need to ask it of you. That is quite clear, is it not ?
And what should make him want your love ? Your
services to him ? Why you have done nothing for him.
He has probably done everything for you. Would he
ask your love unless he loved you for your own sake ?
In other words, his heart has already gone out to you
before he could think of asking you to give him your
heart. This fact that a person or a being loves you
gives him the right to make so great a request from you.

Now who are they who have such a right, and do in
effect say to you, " Give me your heart ? " Before I
answer that question I want to be quite sure that you
understand the meaning of " giving your heart." It
means your thought, your attention, your care, your
affection and your will—all these were understood by
the ancient Hebrew by the word " heart," and all these

you are told to give at the request of certain beings, and to direct to objects dear to them.

Who, then, are those who may justly say to you, Give me your heart and everything that word expresses ?

In the first place surely it is those whose child, whose son or daughter you are, your parents. Has not their heart already gone out to you ? Long before you can remember yourselves, when you were utterly helpless, when if you had been left to yourselves for a day you would have perished, when you were not in the least interesting, but rather a nuisance to other people, their heart was given to you. Even to this very day, when you are little more than a collection of wants, their heart has been given to you. And after to-day, for years before you can be of very much good, it will be given to you. Surely they have the right to ask for your heart.

There is a curious story told in the Talmud of two sons —one used to feed his father on the finest poultry, and, says the Talmud, his punishment will be terrible hereafter ; the other once put his father to grind at the mill, and he will go to Heaven. Very strange, is it not ? But this is what happened. The son who used to give his father fat poultry to eat was one day asked by his father, "My son, whence hast thou obtained these birds ?" and the only answer he gave was, " Eat and devour the lot, like the dogs, and ask no questions." For his heartless speech and unfilial manner he would be punished one day, despite all his fine poultry. And the other who put his father to toil at the mill, why should he be rewarded ? Well that happened so. One day while the lad was grinding corn at the mill for his father, messengers from the King arrived in the village demanding the services of one able-bodied person from every household

to work in the King's fields. It was cruel work, and the
workers were buffeted and treated with contempt.
So the son said to the father, Father, I am young and
strong, can bear such treatment better than you, I will
go to do the King's hard service, and do you meanwhile
labour at the mill and provide what is necessary for the
support of the household. That son will be found in
Paradise (Jer. Talmud, Peah 1). Don't you see the
difference ? The one son followed, the other despised
the law, " Give me thy heart."

So obvious is this to you all, so certain are you all
that your parents have a right to your heart, that I will at
once pass on to another class who ask for your heart
and have the right to ask it.

For, in the next place it is your teachers who say to
you, Give me thy heart, my son or my daughter as the
case may be, for the teachers in Israel were always
considered like parents. The disciples of a prophet
used to call him their father, as you will remember
Elisha did, when he saw Elijah rising heavenward, and
exclaimed " My father, my father, the chariot of Israel " ;
while the disciples themselves were called the sons of the
prophets. Well, your teachers say to you, Give me your
heart. That is, when you are engaged in those studies
which are the main business of your young lives, put
your whole mind and heart into the work. Don't let
your attention be distracted from the one thing on which
for the time being you ought to be employed. I hope I
need not tell you that when you are at play you should
put your whole mind and heart into that, but I fear that
it *is* necessary to caution you to be equally in earnest
when you are, or are supposed to be, at work.

I happen to know a boy—in fact I know several, but I

won't speak about them, for that would take us too far ;
but I will tell you about one, and the way he sets about
his lessons. After a copious tea, which has taken rather
longer than necessary, he will sit down to his work with
all his books and materials around him. But he has no
sooner opened at the right place than he discovers that
a little more ink would be an advantage. He rises to
find the large ink-bottle, in doing so he notices a book
or a paper which he has or has not previously had in
his hands : in either case his thirst for stray information
is aroused, and he reads with much eagerness therein
for a while ; then he remembers that he *must* get on
with his set task, but somehow he cannot settle down ;
he sees a fly moving at ten yards distance ; he hears the
domestic cat gliding through the room ; he is aware
that there has been a knock or a ring at the door, that
visitors are about—a brother or a sister comes in, they are
not sworn to silence ; so the time goes on, and after five
minutes given to one task, four to the next, and three
to the next, his day's work comes to an abrupt close.
I say no word about the accident to the ink-bottle and
the inkstand, about the discovery that the books he
most wanted could not be found in the house, even after
half an hour's searching and loss of temper, for the simple
reason that they were left at school, or about the argument he holds with himself as to which lesson he shall
leave to the last. But I think I have said enough for
you to see that that boy's heart is not in the work he
has to do. If he does not mend his ways, he will not do
much good. If he happens to be here, let him take
warning.

Pray do not imagine that this is simply matter for
laughter. It is a most cruel thing, this waste of the

early life of a child ; and it is more than waste of time, because it means also a loss of brain power as well. Boys and girls lose the habit, or they never acquire it, of fixing their attention on anything, and the more that is neglected when you are young the harder it is to get into the habit as years go on. The Rabbis had a good saying that even a person who is walking on the way and studying,—when you know it is harder to keep your attention steady,—but even such a person, who studies as he walks along, and interrupts himself every now and then and says, " What a lovely tree, what a fine field," is as if he had forfeited his life—indeed part of it he has certainly forfeited and will never get back, because in doing two things at once he has lost the right way of doing either.

You must learn to keep your thoughts well in hand ; to hinder their wandering about. Your tasks for the present at least lie very close at hand ; give your heart to them, my son. " Wisdom," so we read in Solomon's proverbs, " is right before the man of understanding, but the eyes of a fool are in the ends of the earth."

A great schoolmaster used to say that the difference in intellect was very slight among boys—the difference was made visible according as they did or did not put their heart into their work.

But it is especially God who speaks to you in these words—" Give me thy heart, my child." He certainly will accept no work, no gift, no prayer from us in which the heart is not ; He rejects none in which it is. One of our wise men has said : that when a person is truly in earnest and devout, if he comes before God in prayer, though he be ignorant and backward, his mistakes, his stammerings in prayer are to God but signals of his love, and He welcomes them, for has he not given the best thing he possesses—his heart?

Do you know who lately have been giving their heart to God, giving their heart and soul to God? It is those brothers and sisters of ours, your and my brothers and sisters, who have been butchered and burnt to death for God's sake. They have indeed loved Him, for how can one show love more than by giving up one's life for Him whom we love?

It is related in the Talmud that when the great Rabbi Akiba was led forth by the Romans to torture and death, his pupils gathered round him, and mourned over him, saying: Is this the reward for thy devotion to God and His Law? But Rabbi Akiba hushed them and said: My children, all my life long I have prayed for the opportunity to serve God with all my heart and soul and might; with all my heart and soul, even if He take my soul, I have longed for a chance to show my love. And now, shall I be sorry, when God has at last given me the opportunity?

So these people, men, women, and children, very many of them have died in their love of God. They have given their heart, their soul, their life to Him. Now God does not ask us here to give such proof. But He asks our heart still. How can we give it Him? There are many ways. One in particular, by giving it to His suffering children. You cannot love your Father in Heaven unless you love His children on earth.

And here an idea occurs to me. There are I do not know how many scores of children here this morning. You have all of you heard of the sufferings of the Jews in Russia. Do you know that there are hundreds, perhaps thousands, of children of your age and younger whose fathers and mothers have been slaughtered, and who have been left without food, clothing and shelter and without any relative to provide these for them. Many people are trying to help them. But would it not be a glorious thing if every one of you were to give say one penny each for the fund ? Give it to your teachers at school, and ask them to send these pennies to the general fund, but especially for the benefit of the orphan boys and girls. Let those children feel that you have given them your heart because they are your brothers and sisters, being like us all children of God our heavenly Father. It is not much perhaps—a penny—but God does not judge us by much or little, but by the best we are able. " Charity is like a coat of mail," say our sages. You know how a coat of mail is made, little rings each weak in itself but altogether so strong that spears and arrows cannot pierce the coat made of them.

But this is only an occasional means of showing your love. I would have you remember the everyday opportunities which occur to you all. Give your heart to your work ; give your heart to those who love you. Unless you give them your heart, you make a poor return to those who love you ; if you leave their hearts empty nothing else can fill the void. It is wonderful how they go on loving you even if you are ungrateful. But will you be satisfied only to be loved and never to love in return ? No ! You will give your heart to them, and their hearts will be filled with unspeakable joy. They ask no other return for all their sacrifice and efforts. And they will be happy if they get this return. What other return can you make ? Say to them : Mother, father, teacher, God, you ask for my heart, behold I give it to you. And when you say it, mean it.

HE DESPISETH NOT ANY

(*New West End Synagogue,*
Sabbath, October 10th, 1903.)

JOB xxxvi. 5 : " For God is mighty and despiseth not any."

THAT is very good news, dear children, for all of us. God is so great that if we had not been taught otherwise we might perhaps think—He is too great to take any notice of us, to care about what we do ; He is so high above us, He is so mighty that He will pass us over, for what are we in comparison with the Mighty, the Almighty ? But in truth that is His greatness, that none is too great or too small for Him to note, and to love.

I have heard of a little child whom some one was trying to puzzle about his religion, and who was asked : Tell me now, is the God you believe in a great God, or a little God ; and the child paused for a moment and said : Both—so great that He fills the whole world, and so little that He can come into my heart. For God is mighty and despiseth not any.

Even the people we might think He would despise He doesn't. He may be displeased with them ; He may punish them ; He may even be sorry for them— but how can He despise any creature of His almighty hand ?

Or we might, if we were not better taught, imagine that it is vain to think of serving God unless we can do something wonderful and startling—unless we were among the great ones of the land—that for quite ordinary people like ourselves He will have no regard. But the Bible teaches us otherwise. " I dwell in the high and holy place—and with him also that is of a lowly and contrite spirit." There is nothing wonderful and startling in that—only just true simplicity and earnestness of heart.

Or we might say : What can a child do or say that shall please the great and mighty God ? Grown up people are different. But a child ? Well—it is especially to the child that the Bible speaks. " Remember the Creator in the days of thy youth."

Just as He will not despise any one, so He will not despise anything if offered to Him with the sincere purpose of honouring Him therewith. What a lesson on that subject our present festival teaches ! For instance, we are to serve Him in our synagogues and our homes, which you know are solid and sometimes even splendid buildings ; but equally He is served by us in the Succah whose roof is of leaves that wither and fade away after a week or so. So also we honour Him at this season by rejoicing before Him with plants of various sorts— they may bear goodly fruit or smell sweetly, or do neither ; and one is of the tallest of trees, the palm ; and another, the citron, is of those that never reach a great height ; and one remains green all the year round, the myrtle ; and another the willow, sheds its leaves and becomes bare every winter. But God despiseth not any.

Now everything we learn about the goodness of God is intended for a double purpose. First, to make us revere and love Him, so that we think and behave reverently in His presence ; and then to get us to imitate Him, as far as we can. God is a Father who loves His children, and not only likes to have them about Him, but wants them to show their love for Him by working with Him—that is, with and for one another. And so we also must strive to copy Him and despise not any.

It is one of the faults we have to guard against, young and old, that we do not get into the way of thinking contemptuously of others who happen to be differently made or differently gifted from ourselves. God's gifts are bestowed in various ways. He does not give all things to any one person, but to the one he grants one sort of favour and to the other another, so that none shall complain, and none have the right to lord it over others and despise them.

Did you ever hear the fable told by Bowden of the stage-coach and the milestone ? You know, of course, what a milestone is ; it is a stone placed on the high-road and marks the number of miles from a certain place, so that travellers may always know how far they have gone or how far they have to go. And a stage-coach is a sort of glorified omnibus—there were more of that sort in former days before railroads and steam engines were invented. Well, a stage-coach one day was stopping for a few minutes near an old milestone, and it looked at the stone and laughed in a conceited way quite aloud, and said to the milestone, " Look at us, we travel far and we travel fast, but you—aren't you tired of always standing in one place ? " " If you are not tired with running," answered the old milestone, " why should I be of staying ? " " Ah, but I am on wheels, and my duties require nimbleness," remarked the coach.

" Granted," replied the milestone, " but I don't see there is so great a difference between us, after all. You would be as motionless as myself without your horses ; and as to usefulness, milestones have their uses as well as stage-coaches. If yours are to carry passengers from place to place, mine are to afford the travellers information on their way. Besides, boast as you may, I have sometimes heard of coaches upsetting, and break- ing down, and wearing out, and being stopped and robbed " (that was in the old days), " but I never heard of such things happening to milestones. Therefore, friend, taking all things into consideration, I fancy I am the safer if the quieter of the two ; and if you are happy in running, I am contented in staying humbly to do the duties of my station ; and perhaps as honour- ably as yourself, although you are a fast coach and myself am but a poor milestone on the road." All have their places in the world, and the great question for every one of us is now, and by and by will be : How do we fill the place for which we have been selected ? Are we doing the best we can with the gifts God has bestowed upon us ? I hope we are, and if we are we shall be less inclined than ever to despise others.

Yes the gifts of God are very rarely granted in great number to any one person—perhaps because it would make them too conceited. For instance, beauty and wisdom do not always go together. But it would be a foolish person who despised another because she or he had the one quality and not the other.

It is related in the Talmud (Taanith 7a) of a certain Rabbi—Joshua ben Chananya—that he was very highly esteemed on account of his wisdom at the court of the Roman Emperor. But a regard for truth com-

pelled people to admit that he was not equally remarkable for personal beauty. One day the Emperor's
daughter happened to pass him in the palace, and she
was so struck by the Rabbi's ugliness that before she
knew it, unaccustomed to govern her tongue, she blurted
out, " What a hideous vessel to contain all that wisdom." (It was, as a little girl to whom I once told the
tale said, most unprincessly of her to talk like that.)

But the Rabbi, being, as I have said, a wise man,
wasn't a bit offended, and seemed to take no notice
of the unprincessly remark. Instead of that he entered
into conversation with her about all sorts of things.
"Tell me," he said, "Princess, in what sort of vessels does
his august majesty, your father, keep his wine ? "
" In what sort of vessels ? " she replied ; " why, in
earthen vessels." " What," he exclaimed, " your
imperial father, the lord of the Roman Empire, puts
his wine in earthenware casks ; why, that's what the
commonest people do : he ought to keep wine in vessels
of silver and gold." " Well," said the princess, " there
does seem something in what you say." And forthwith
she went and gave orders to empty all the wine in the
imperial cellars from earthenware into gold and silver
vessels.

Shortly afterwards the Emperor gave a banquet,
ordered some of his famous wines to be brought for the
enjoyment of his guests. What was their surprise to
find that cask after cask was sour—all the wine, in fact,
had turned sour. He sent for the butler, and he said
it was the princess's fault ; he sent for the princess, and
she put the blame upon the Rabbi. Then the Rabbi
was fetched. " What is the meaning of this ? " " Sire,"
replied the Rabbi, " I only wanted to teach the princess

a lesson. Your daughter had much too high an opinion of mere outside beauty—she despised me because of my unsightly face and figure. It was necessary that she should know that wisdom and beauty are not often combined—and she has learned that lesson now in the form of a parable she is not likely to forget." " But surely there have been handsome men who have also been learned and wise ? " " True," replied the Rabbi ; " still I think that if they had been less handsome they would have been more wise."

It is a curious thing that the very wisest man among the ancient Greeks—and one of the noblest characters that ever lived—Socrates—was extremely ugly. Still there was a charm about him that, wherever he appeared, conquered all hearts. Once his enemies made fun of him at the theatre, and made up a man on the stage like him, who mimicked him, and everybody laughed. But all at once Socrates himself came into the theatre, and stood among the people, and when they beheld the real man they felt ashamed of themselves, and stopped the fooling.

Of course you will not be so foolish as to think that all beautiful people must be silly, and all ugly ones wise. Wisdom and folly are not to be detected by such a mechanical outside test. Wisdom is an inward grace and beauty an outward one ; the one is not always present when the other is absent. Both may be there, just as neither may be there.

One man there was, the wisest who ever lived, who was also most beautiful. That was Moses. They say he was a lovely baby, and that when he was born the whole house was filled with light. But he could have both these qualities without their hurting him. Why ?

Because he was not conceited ; because he was also at the same time the meekest and most humble man upon the face of the earth. When he had been speaking with God it is said that he came forth with his face shining, giving out rays of light. All the people saw it, and were in awe of him ; the only man who did not know that his face shone was Moses himself. It was his modesty that made his beauty more beautiful, and his wisdom more wise. He, too, mighty as he was by reason of his great gifts, despised not any, but loved all his people, in spite of all the differences for good or evil that were among them.

But especially, dear children, be on your guard lest you despise any because of some physical defect they may have—in speech or movement—which is not their fault. Children are sometimes rather cruel and inconsiderate in this way. It is that they don't think ; but it gives pain all the same—to be despised for anything, particularly if it's for something one can't help. It is not only mean and cruel, it is positively absurd. Who are *we* that we should despise others ? Has not every one of us not one but many defects ? Instead of despising other people, we should rather try to make ourselves less despicable. And one of the best and noblest ways to do this is to be kind and helpful to those whom we are in a position to befriend.

One of the most wonderful stories ever told is that which has recently been printed in a book called *The Story of my Life,* a book written—just think of it—by a young woman named Helen Keller, who is blind and deaf. When she was less than two years old she had a terrible illness and lost sight and hearing. But she had sensible parents and a loving and patient and wise teacher, and so bit by bit, by the sense of touch alone, she has learnt to read and write, and even learned several languages, and all her ideas have grown. She has learned to speak by the movement of her lips ; she can tell what others say by placing her finger on their lips, and instead of remaining in darkness and dulness and misery all her life, she has become a highly educated and intelligent young woman, who can write books which very few persons with all their senses complete could produce. Of course God has been kind to her by making her sense of touch so quick and fine that it makes up to a great extent for the senses of hearing and seeing which she has lost.

But what would she have been if it had not been for the loving patience of her friend and instructress, who had to teach her everything from the beginning with infinite trouble, and who never lost hope, and has at length been rewarded. That was doing God's work, for He despiseth not any.

Not all of us indeed can devote our lives to such a cause or to one person ; but every time, dear children, you do something to help the weak, or to comfort those that are in trouble, or to give joy to those that are sad, especially when you give your loving care and kindness to those whom the world doesn't care for, doesn't love or doesn't think of much account, who are plain and unattractive, and poor and not likely to make you any return for your pains—you are doing God's work. The beautiful, and the graceful, and the clever and gifted, and the lucky, and the rich—they have plenty of friends. It is those who lack all these advantages that want friends ; and if you have the power and you resolve to be their friend, you will assuredly be doing the work of God, who is mighty and despiseth not any.

EBB AND FLOW

(New West End Synagogue,
Tabernacles, October 14th, 1905.)

ECCLESIASTES i. 7 : " All the rivers run into the seâ, yet the sea is not full ; unto the place whither the rivers go, thither they go again."

THE wise man who wrote the book of Ecclesiastes is describing in this passage some of the wonderful ways in which nature works. First he speaks of the sun. It rises in the east and sets in the west regularly, and having done so, it hasteth or panteth—that is a poetical way of expressing it—it panteth to come back where it started from, in order to start again, and go on its circuit—and so east and west and west and east are ever being connected. Then there are the winds. They blow towards the south, then veer round until they blow in the opposite direction, and then after a while repeat the same round. Then there are the rivers. Water, as you have been taught at school, seeks its lowest level, so the rivers flow down, down—all of them—into the sea. But the sea doesn't overflow the land, for the large surface of water gives off an enormous amount of vapour ; this rises, gets carried away by the currents of wind in the upper parts, and is condensed in the higher, colder regions to fall down again as rain, or perhaps as snow on tops of mountains, which flows into brooks, and these into rivers, and these again into the sea—and so the whole process begins again, and so on and so on, seemingly without end.

Now what may we learn from all this ? First, of course, the wonderful order of nature, which under God's commands continues to-day just as it did thousands of years ago. So also the seasons go on regularly—spring, summer, autumn, which we have now, and winter—none of them lasting too long, never stopping in their round, each season coming back in its turn at the bidding of God. The Bible tells us that God Himself promised this : "While the earth remaineth, seed-time and harvest, cold and heat, summer and winter, and day and night shall not cease " (Genesis viii. 22). How great must He be who set all these things in motion and keeps them so with unbroken regularity, and how well we do to give utterance to the thanks of our heart for each in turn as it comes round, as we do on this very Festival of Ingathering, when we thank Him who has promised and has kept His promise to bless us in all our produce and in all the work of our hands, so that we may be indeed joyful.

But we may learn something else from our text. It is that all things belong together, they depend upon on another, that nothing is by itself and for itself, but each for all and all for each. All the rivers flow to the sea, the sea exists by reason of the rivers that fill it, and the rivers exist because of the sea which not only receives water, but gives it back in the form of vapour. And so everything is kept in continual motion, and is clean and healthy.

You have often been into the Park and into Kensington Gardens, and have seen the Round Pond and the

Serpentine. Haven't you noticed how clean they always are ? I wonder if you have ever asked yourselves how is it that they never grow stagnant. Well, the explanation is very simple. If you look closely, you will find that water is always flowing in and flowing out. It looks quite still, but it is always really on the move, receiving and giving. If the waters did not do that they would soon become stagnant and putrid and unpleasant, but they are instead always clear and sweet. They do not make a great noise about it, but they are clear and sweet for all that, and they are so because they are always receiving and giving.

Is not that a lesson to us all ? A lesson that we must not only receive but give, not only get from others but grant to others. For no single human soul is by itself and for itself alone. There is a beautiful saying in the Midrash : In Nature there is always lending and borrowing — the day borrows from the night and the night from the day; that is, the day doesn't pass into night in a single instant, nor the night into day—it isn't one moment bright sunshine and the next black darkness — but there is twilight, when the day gradually passes into night, and dawn, when the night slowly passes away and gives way to light—a beautiful as well as a loving arrangement of things ; and again, the earth borrows from the heavens and the heavens from the earth—for there is sunshine, and dew, and rain, which come from above, and there are those beautiful clouds and colours in the sky which, I am sure, you have often wondered at, and which are caused—by what do you think ?—by the small particles of dust that float in the air in myriads, though you cannot see them with the naked eye. " Wisdom borrows from knowledge, and knowledge from wisdom "—that is, the more wise we are the more we shall wish to know, and the more we know the wiser we shall be. Justice borrows from mercy and mercy from justice, i.e. you can't be truly merciful unless you strive also to be just ; and you can't be perfectly just unless you are also merciful, for man's justice is then most like God's

> When mercy seasons justice.

So all things lend to and borrow from each other. Should we be the only creatures of God to forget that we must not only take favours but bestow them, not only receive love but give it ?

Depend upon it, kindness begets kindness, and unkindness, unkindness.

I have heard an odd story about a couple of young men who were students at one college in Oxford. They were acquaintances—I cannot say they were friends—and their rooms were at some little distance from one another. I don't want to mention names—real names—so I will call them Brown and Jones. One day Brown, who had not been working very hard except at sports, had a great deal of Latin to get through, and couldn't find his Latin dictionary. So he sent a messenger across to Jones, who had a very good Latin dictionary, with the request, Would Jones lend it to him. Jones sent back this note : " My dear Brown, I never lend my dictionary out of my room ; but if you like to come over you can use it here." Brown felt hurt. The next day happened to be very cold and men had their fires lighted. Jones had his lighted too, but the fire was burning low— he couldn't find the poker which had somehow disappeared. So he sent a message across to Brown—

" Would he be good enough to lend Jones his poker ? "
Brown thereupon wrote this answer : " My dear Jones,
I never lend the poker out of my room, but if you like to
come across here you can poke my fire for me."

Now I haven't the least doubt that every one of you
will say, " Serve Jones right ; he shouldn't have been
so disagreeable." And that is so. There can be no
doubt that it did serve Jones right, and it was a rather
funny retaliation. But do you not think that they were
both rather disagreeable ? Don't you think that, unless
Jones had been a very bad-hearted or a very thick-
headed fellow, it would have done more good if Brown
had lent him that poker right away ? I fancy Jones
would have been a good deal ashamed of himself when
he reflected to himself, Here am I receiving a favour
from some one to whom I refused a favour—I must go
and beg his pardon, and make up for my churlishness in
some way. As it was they fell out, and I am not sure if
they speak to each other to this day.

However, the main point is to understand that in this
life if you want to be treated as a brother you must
behave as one.

There are some good lines by a great German poet,
Goethe, which I try to translate thus :

> With pockets tightly closed, my brother,
> Thou hopest favours to receive.
> One hand is washed but by another ;
> If thou wouldst take, then thou must give.

Now just apply this to your own case, dear children.
You live, say, in a house where there are others besides
yourself. Indeed, if you were alone you would be very
miserable, it would be no home at all to you. Well, if
you want other people, your brothers and sisters, your

parents and friends to consider you, you must consider them. And so at school. It is very nice to be top of your class, as I daresay some of you are. But there is something better than being first in cleverness—it is better to be first in kindness. It is better for others, it is better for you, for kindness is twice blessed. It blesses the giver, it blesses the receiver.

Sometimes, indeed, the return is not rapid. It may take a long time to come back to us. Or it may not come back to us ourselves at all, but to those who come after us. Well, what of that ? Do not we enjoy many, many blessings which have come down to us from those who have long ago passed away, whom we never even knew ? All progress is bit by bit, and we reap what others sow. What should we know of our religion to-day, if it hadn't been for the strong faith of our fathers of long ago ? Did they think of themselves alone when they clung to their religion, with all their soul's strength ?

There is a story told in the Talmud of an old man who was seen planting a tree which only bears fruit after seventy years. Some one was watching him, and seeing him engaged in a task from which he was not likely ever to obtain any benefit said to him : " What useless work is this thou art doing ; dost thou hope to live to reap any fruit from it ? " " My friend," replied the aged man, " I found the world provided with such trees. They were planted by my fathers, and I have enjoyed the fruit of them. As my fathers planted for me, so I plant for those that come after me."

And that, dear children, is the real way to do good. No love is ever wasted—not even the wish to act lovingly is wasted. All the rivers, big and little, run into the sea. Do you think a drop of it all is wasted ?

No, indeed it is not. Not even the vapour into which that drop is changed ; for one day—it may be long after it has floated about the air seemingly without aim— it will be met by a particular current of air and it will be changed back into water, and will descend as rain and fall into some stream which will carry it into the great sea which keeps our whole world clean and fresh and healthy.

Now, dear children, after the service is over you are also to receive something. You will receive—unless you have a rooted objection to such things—a welcome in the tabernacle, with something added. I should be sorry to think that that is the reason you have come here this morning, but you shall receive it all the same. Only you will remember that you have to give something as well—to give your minds to try and understand how great the mercy of God has been in preserving you, after all these thousands of years, as Jews ; you have to give your soul in thanks, your heart in sympathy and kindness to all you meet, especially those less fortunate than yourselves. Never fear that it will be wasted, for it is these things which, like rivers, make the land habitable, and like the sea, keep the whole world clean, fresh and healthy.

BIRDS AND THEIR WAYS

*(New West End Synagogue,
Seventh Day of Passover, April 25th,* 1903.)

Song of Solomon ii. 12 : " The time of the singing of birds is come, and the voice of the turtle dove is heard in our land."

THE man who wrote this beautiful poem, which it is usual to read on Passover, the spring festival, had his eyes and ears open, and, better still, his heart open, to every lovely thing in nature. When you are older you may be able to understand that poem better than you can now, or than any one can at present teach you.

But what you can understand now is his description of spring—so simple and so charming. " Rise up," he says, " my love, my fair one, and come away," or come out and see for yourself. " For behold the winter is past, the rain is over and gone ; the flowers appear on the earth ; the time of the singing of birds is come, and the voice of the turtle dove is heard in our land." It is upon the last part that I want you to fix your attention, because I wish to speak to you a little this morning about birds and some of the lessons we may learn from them.

I trust you all love birds, though I hope you do not love them, as so many people do, in your hats. I want you to love them for themselves and for what they tell you, and not to be among those who, in order to deck themselves up in rare and most exquisite feathers, do not mind if whole families of some of the loveliest of God's creatures be killed off from the face of the earth.

The next time you go to the Natural History Museum in South Kensington I want you to look especially at a couple of birds. Formerly they were difficult to see : they used to be upstairs, and to get at them you had to pass the refreshment room ; and I often noticed that children once near the refreshment room forgot all about the birds. Well, as you go in you turn to the gallery immediately at your left. It is full of specimens of birds of the most beautiful colour and shape. Go past them all right to the end of the gallery, where there are a few cases of British birds. In one of those cases are a couple of birds which you will very likely miss unless you take care to find them. Lots of people never see them. The little creature is nothing much to look at, it isn't very much larger than a well grown London sparrow, it is very soberly coloured, not a bit showy, quite a plainly dressed little thing. Yet that simple, dull coloured bird is worth remembering. Of all the birds in the museum there was none who in life could sing like that bird. It is the nightingale, whose sweetly plaintive song has touched the hearts of all men in all ages. So much so that there used to be a fable about it, that it went up to a thorn, pressed the thorn into its little breast, and that the pain it thus suffered caused it to sing those ringing, tender notes by which it is known. That story isn't true, of course ; but what is true is—that you cannot go by appearances. The peacock is a splendid looking bird, but, oh ! what a voice it has ! As you grow older people will probably judge you not by your looks, but by what you are and what you can do, and it is well, dear children, that you should prepare at once for that time.

Then there is another bird in the same gallery you ought to look for, though that also is not much to look at. It is the lark. Next to the nightingale perhaps the lark has the most glorious voice. But another thing. If I remember rightly there is a model of the kind of nest the lark builds. It usually builds its nest on the ground, but when it sings it rises higher and higher in the sky until the eye tries in vain to follow it, and all we know is that a stream of melody pours down from somewhere in the heavens. That bird that rises higher almost than any other has its nest on the earth. It is a humble bird. And the nightingale, when may its voice be heard ? In the evening and through the night. It never shows itself. Cannot those little creatures teach us something ? Have you ever heard the lines :—

> The bird that soars on highest wing
>   Builds on the ground her lowly nest,
> And she that doth most sweetly sing,
>   Sings in the shade when all things rest.
> In lark and nightingale we see
>   What honour hath humility.

Very few birds sing as well in captivity as when they are free. Some will not sing at all if you put them in a cage. They are longing for liberty, I suppose, and their hearts are too full for songs. It is a curious thing —which the older ones among you will perhaps have noticed—that the account of the song of Moses and the Israelites which we read to-day, because it was on this seventh day of Passover that they crossed the Red Sea and Pharaoh and his hosts troubled them no more, that that song is introduced in these words : " Then sang Moses." That is, after they had gone forth into freedom, then and not till then could they sing. They do not seem to have sung while they were in slavery. They could not sing. Only when they were set free they sang, and very well, too, a song of praise to God. And many hundreds of years afterwards, when they went into captivity in Babylon, and their masters asked them to sing some songs of Zion for the amusement of their captors, they could not do it ; they hung up their harps upon the trees by the rivers of Babylon—" How shall we sing the songs of Zion in a strange land ? " But when that time was over " and the Lord brought the captives back " we read, " Then was our mouth full of mirth and our tongue with joyous song."

Well, dear children, we are free in this country, perfectly free, and if ever there was a people that ought to sing praise to God, it is the Jews of England—little and big. That is one reason why you are so welcome to come to Synagogue, or to go to the children's services that you may sing to God along with others of the children of Israel, because you are free. And even if you cannot sing well that doesn't matter so much. I have read of a little girl who, as she was going to bed, heard the sound of young ravens cawing aloud in the trees close by. " Do you know what that is ? " said her mother to her. " Yes, mother," she replied, " that's the young ravens saying their prayers." She was a very little child, and she probably didn't know that she said almost exactly what the Bible says, " He giveth food to the young ravens who call upon Him."

Then, further, we might learn a lesson of self-depen-
dence from birds. Of course birds should be kindly
treated ; but if you do too much for them they don't
like it, and they won't accept it. There was once a
man who had lots of money and very little brains, and
he put up a magnificent aviary—a big bird-cage. He
liked to be comfortable, and he would make his birds
comfortable. He wanted to improve birds by sparing
them trouble, and so at nesting time he had a number
of nests made, beautifully made, all ready for the birds.
He then put in a lot of birds, wrens, and thrushes, and
chaffinches, and tomtits, and I don't know what. No
sooner, however, had the little things got inside than
they pulled all the things to pieces and set about building and furnishing on their own account.

You remember the dove that flew out of Noah's ark
and back again with an olive leaf in its mouth. Well,
there is a legend that that leaf was plucked from a tree in
Paradise ; yet it was a bitter leaf, and when Noah asked
the dove, "Why have you got this bitter leaf," the
dove answered, "Better the bitter at the hand of God
than the sweet at the hand of man."

And that should be your principle, especially you boys
when you grow older ; when you begin to fly for yourself, strive to be independent, though the experience
be bitter at first. Strive to use the opportunities God
has given you rather than depend upon the constant aid
of others.

One of the most beautiful things in the world it is
to notice the love and tender care shown to the young
by the parent birds. Very often both the father and
the mother bird work together in preparing the nest,
and while the mother sits on the egg or keeps the little

birds warm the father forages about for food for them all. With some birds, the puffin, for instance, the father digs a tortuous burrow ten feet deep in the earth ready for the eggs. At the Natural History Museum you may see models, copied from nature, of these things. Even geese and turkeys know how to protect their young, as some of you may have found out. All signs of love in animals make us love them more and increase our love for one another. Are lower creatures to be better than we ?

Then again there are many species of birds who live together and seek their food together and wander away together in companies. Such are the fieldfares, starlings and swallows, and especially the rooks. Do you know that rooks when they are feeding put one of their number to watch to let the rest know if danger is coming ? It is his business to give them a signal in rookish, which is the language they all understand, and when they get the warning they fly off in the opposite direction. I have read in a book by an eminent naturalist that if the sentinel rook fails in his duty the others judge him and peck him to death. And it is even said that if the young birds when they build their nest for the first time go and steal twigs from other nests instead of collecting them, they are soon taught a lesson, for the older birds unite to tear their nests to pieces until they have learned to do their own work honestly. On the other hand, rooks and terns, or sea swallows, have been known to feed a blind or wounded fellow-bird, and try to save him when caught in a snare or seriously hurt.

Sometimes, you know, birds bring up a little brood of young that do not properly belong to them, and perhaps do not even belong to their own species. Hens will sit on eggs they have never laid, and they will hatch them out, and then they will love the young chicks as if they were their own ; they will keep them warm and feed them, and protect them from enemies, and mother them in every way, and, in fact, give them a regular bird education.

Something of that sort happens among human beings too. People have sometimes adopted other people's children, and have been to them as good as their own mothers and fathers could have been. There is, for instance, our Jews' Hospital and Orphan Asylum. That is an institution which takes care of and mothers and trains all the poor children who have lost father and mother, or whose parents, through some terrible misfortune not their own fault, are disabled from doing by them a parent's part. What a blessed thing that is. I wonder if there are any children here who do not belong to our Children's Orphan Aid Society, or, if they do, have forgotten to pay their penny a week. If you want to know all about it send me a post card. But there is one thing especially that I want you to do. When you go home I want you to say to your mother and father, and to the friends who love you best, Have you given something this year to the Orphan Asylum ? Yes ? If so, have you given enough ? Yes ? If so, give something for my sake. I don't think they will refuse you.

One of the most marvellous things about birds is what is called their migration. They will appear at one place where they can get their food, where they will build their nests, and rear their young, then after a while they disappear, go to some place, it may be, thousands of miles away, and come again back to the old place next year. What is it that teaches them the road ? Some go in whole flocks, but some go single, high up in the air, and often in the dark, over seas more than a thousand miles. How can they do it ? How do they know the way ? Some say it is instinct, which is a way of saying they do not understand. Call it what you will, it is very wonderful, and if God did not give them the knowledge or the power they never could take those journeys, and they would soon die out. The prophet Jeremiah knew all about this " migration." He says that the stork in the heaven knoweth her appointed time, and the turtle dove, the crane and the swallow know the time of their coming—but my people know not the ordinance of the Lord. We ought not, dear children, to be too proud to learn from birds.

There is a story of a Saxon chief who was sitting one dark evening with his vassals and thralls in a hall that was lighted and warmed by a great log fire, and they were talking about serious things. Suddenly there flew into the hall through a crevice at one end a little bird. For a little while the bird circled round the hall, then at a crevice in the opposite wall he flew out. Behold, said the chief to his followers, a picture of human life. Out of the darkness into the light, out again into the darkness. What he meant was, we do not know what we were before we came into the world ; we do not know what we shall be after we go out of it— there is light and warmth here in this life for a little while—before and after all is darkness. He spoke like that because he knew no other—but you and I have been better taught. I suppose he did not think that the bird had his nest somewhere outside, or that perhaps he was making his way to a great distance to some sunnier and brighter land where his home was and it would be well with him.

And so we, dear children, we need not fear. He who teaches the bird to find his way across seas and mountains—high up beyond where our eyes can follow him—and in the dark—He will not forsake us, His children. When we go out into the dark He will be our guardian and our guide to a happier home than ever was ours in the brightest and happiest spot on earth. So you see the birds teach us this thing also, to trust in God even to the end, even to the end.

KINDNESS TO ANIMALS

(New West End Synagogue, 1902.)

PSALM cxlvii. 9 : " He giveth to the beast his food,and to the young ravens which cry."

THERE was an ancient idea that though grown-up ravens were fond of one another—for " birds of a feather flock together "—yet the old ravens, it was believed, did not love the young. Young ravens have not yet got their black plumage, they are not yet " birds of a feather." So it was believed that ravens turned their young out of their nests so early that the poor little creatures were not yet strong and wise enough to get food for themselves. Hence it was thought that when the Psalmist wished to tell how God provides for all His creatures, the writer particularly mentioned young ravens, because they so much needed His help. For the good name of the raven family, one is glad to hear that naturalists no longer believe this unkind story about ravens and their young. What made the Psalmist specially think of ravens was this. You know how often and how persistently ravens croak. They seem always a little impatient and angry, as if they were hungry and very badly wanted something to eat.

There are many other passages in the Bible in which

we are told of God's love for all animals. " God causeth
the grass to grow for the cattle, and herb (that is all
vegetable products) for the labour of man." Do you
notice the difference ? The grass grows for the cattle,
but the vegetables need human labour if they are to be
used for man. But think only of the first point ; how
God provides for all animals. Later on in the same
104th Psalm, we are told about the birds who
make their nests in the cedars of Lebanon, the
storks who live in the tall fir-trees, the wild goat or
ibex and the coney who lives on the high hills and in
the rocks. The ibex " lives in holes in the rocks, where
it makes its nest and conceals its young, and to which
it retires at the least alarm." I have taken this last
sentence from Tristram's *Natural History of the
Bible,* a book which you must all read when you are a
little older. It is very interesting, but a little too hard
for you at present. Well, the Psalmist goes on to
speak even of beasts of prey. The young lions roar,
and " seek their food from God." The Psalmist had
just before spoken of the " Birds that sing among the
branches "—so peacefully—and now of the lions who
roar so noisily for their prey. Even these fierce beasts
are under God's control. We do not always know what
such animals are good for, but we may be sure that God
knows. The Psalmist at all events has a heart wide
enough to contain all of God's creatures, he loves them
all. And so, after mentioning so many kinds of animals,
some living on the land and some in the water, he says :
" All of these wait upon Thee, and Thou givest them
their food in due season. What Thou givest unto them
they gather, Thou openest thy hand, they are satisfied
with good." And so we need not wonder then, in

another Psalm (xxxvi.), all this is summed up in the beautiful sentence : " O Lord, Thou preservest man and beast."

Now, I need hardly tell Jewish boys and girls that they must always be kind to animals. Our whole Bible is full of love for the lower creatures. You remember how the servant of Abraham chose a wife for Isaac. He did not ask if she was rich, or beautiful, but whether she was kind to animals. When Rebekah said : " I will draw water for thy camels also," thinking of the hard-working thirsty animals who do so much for men in the desert lands—when she said this, he knew that he had found a bride of the most lovely character. Then think of two of the greatest men, Moses and David. Both of them were shepherds. The Midrash tells us that one day a lamb strayed from Jethro's flock. Moses was the shepherd, and he wandered for hours and hours searching for the lost lamb. When he found it, it was so tired that it could not walk, and Moses carried it home in his bosom. Then, the story tells us, God said : You have shown such love for this little lamb, that you are fit to be trusted to guide and lead all the people of Israel.

But you may say, Did not God place all lower animals under our power ? Yes, He did. Man is lord over all other creatures. He may not be so strong as some, nor so fast as others, nor so big as all. But he has the intelligence to master them all. We are masters, but we must not be tyrants. Do you know what a tyrant is ? He is one who never thinks of any one else, but because he has the power, he uses it without feeling ; he is strong and cruel. But we must be strong and kind ; lords and masters, not tyrants over other creatures. We must never make them suffer pain that we can help. We are allowed to kill certain animals for food, but we must be careful to kill them with as little pain to them as we can. Judaism tells us never to cut a limb off a live animal. It is said that there are still cruel tribes that do such things. Then, again, when an ox was treading out the corn he was not allowed to be muzzled. I daresay that you have sometimes been in parts where the oxen are employed in ploughing and other work in the fields. It would be cruel to tie up the animal's mouth, so that he could not now and them eat a little of the corn. Then, again, an ox and an ass were not to be yoked to the same plough. The ox is much stronger, and the ass would be hurt by trying or being forced to do as much work as the stronger animal.

In many other ways the Bible commands us to think of the feelings of animals. We must never neglect them. There is a wonderful commandment: "If thou seest thine enemy's ox or his ass crouching under his burden, thou must surely help him." It is bad enough to have an enemy at all, but we must not be at war also with the ox or the ass of a person who is not friends with us. And then, on the Sabbath day all dumb animals that work for man must rest. The loving God, who is good unto all, and whose mercy is upon all His works, did not forget these when He made the Sabbath day a source of blessing for man and beast alike.

But, in Judaism animals are not only men's servants, they are also his teachers. I have often had occasion to call your attention to the many lessons that animals can teach us. In the Bible, the dove teaches us constancy, the eagle love, the ant industry, the ox gratitude.

And now I come to an even more important point.

The way that we treat animals has an influence on ourselves. Every kind deed you do to an animal makes your own nature kinder and better. Every cruel deed against animals makes your own nature crueller and worse. Animals have sensitive natures; they feel pain and enjoy pleasure. Therefore we have to be kind to them for their own sakes. But it is for our sakes too that we must be kind. "Thou hast made man ruler over the works of Thy hands, hast placed all things under his feet; sheep and oxen all of them; also the beasts of the field, the fowls of the heaven, and the fishes of the sea." So sang the author of the eighth Psalm. But the same Psalm tells us, "Thou hast made man but little lower than the angels, and hast crowned him with honour and glory." Now how can we be said to have a crown of honour if we are cruel to all these animals placed in our power? We become lower than they are if we are unkind to them. "A righteous man knoweth the feelings of his beast," we are told. There is a precept which you all know I am sure, that when we use animals for food, we must not kill the parents and the young in one day. What was the reason for this? Some think that it was to spare the feelings of the parent, who ought not to be forced to see its own young killed before its eyes. But it would be easy to separate them before killing them, or to kill them at different hours in the same day. I do not think, then, that this command has anything to do with the feelings of the animals themselves; it is, as Dr. Jellinek says, meant for *us*, it has to do with *our* feelings. It is a dreadful idea for us to think of mother and young being destroyed in one day. This is what I meant by what I said above. *We* suffer if we are cruel to animals.

Our own nature is made coarse. And more. If we are cruel to lower animals we are cruel to our fellow creatures. The boy who tortures animals will also be unkind to his sisters. We refine our own nature when we are kind, and we spoil our own nature when we are cruel to animals.

Now there are two things in particular that I want to say to my younger hearers. A good deal depends on the way you treat your animal pets, if you do keep any. You must be very careful never to inflict pain on them. You must never neglect them. Some children are unkind without meaning it. Be on your guard against this.

Then, again, never have anything to do with " sport " that is cruel to animals. Fortunately Jews, owing to their religion, are not often guilty of this wickedness. But be watchful that you never join even as lookers-on at cruel pastimes.

I am sure you will not. I am sure that you will never prove false to this, one of the chief teachings of Judaism —the teaching that to inflict pain is one of the worst sins you can commit. And if it be wicked to give pain to a fellow human being, who can to some extent protect himself, is it not wicked to hurt dumb creatures, who cannot speak, but who can feel ? God provides for the young ravens which cry to Him for food. You will show yourselves children of God when you, too, have a heart for all God's creatures, sparing them all un-necessary pain, and giving every thought possible to their feelings and to their needs,

THE LADS' BRIGADE

(*New West End Synagogue,*
Sabbath, July 2nd, 1898.)

Of you, dear brethren, whom I have the privilege of addressing Sabbath after Sabbath, I solicit indulgence if I direct my remarks this morning more particularly to our young friends and visitors who have come here from a considerable distance and to whom and to whose cause we may well offer a cordial welcome.

The formation of the Jewish Lads' Brigade, one detachment of which has marched from the East of London to take part in our service to-day, is a sign and a most pleasing sign, of the progress of that assimilation in the national life of England which all Jews are so desirous of seeing perfected. For this is an assimilation towards the good and the manly, and no Jew of England is a true Jew unless he is not only ready but enthusiastically ready to associate himself with all that part of English life which is at once ennobling to the character and responsive to the Jew's sense of duty to his country.

Numbers xx.17 : "We will go along the King's highway."

THAT was part of the message, as we have read in this morning's lesson, which the Israelites sent to the King and people of Edom. The Israelites were at the latter part of their long wanderings and on the march to the promised land. Their shortest route lay through the land of Edom. Israel and Edom, which, as you know, are the same as Jacob and Esau, had sprung from the same parent stock, but they had parted, and gone different roads, and two nations were now in the place of the two brothers.

To the King of Edom Moses now sends an embassy :
" Thus saith thy brother Israel," they were charged to
address him ; the appeal could be made on no higher
grounds.

Then they were to narrate very briefly, so as not to
weary the listeners, the outlines of Israel's past history,
and to state their plan for the future.   " Let us pass,
we pray, through thy land, we will not pass through
field or vineyard ; neither will we drink of the waters of
the wells on private property, we will go by the King's
highway—(that was the public road constructed at
the cost of the State for the King and his armies to use,
and is said to be the same as the old broad military
roads still found here and there in the east, and known
as the " Sultan " or " Emperor road ").   " On the public road," then, " we will go, and not turn to the right
hand or to the left until we have passed thy borders."
But the King of Edom was in an unbrotherly, suspicious
mood, and would not give them permission to go through
his country.   Once more the Israelites try to soothe
him, assuring him in words very much as before, " we
only want to go up by the highway, and if we drink of
the water, I and my cattle, I will pay for it.   It is nothing that I ask.   I will only go through on my feet."
But all these good words were thrown away, or at least
they seemed so, and Israel had to march a long way
round in order to avoid coming into conflict with Edom.
Whether these good words and good intentions were
really thrown away we shall see by and by ; meanwhile,
what is certain is that they did not effect their object,
and it was in vain that our fathers pleaded, " We will
go by the King's highway."

Now, my dear boys, you must not imagine that that

was the only period when the high roads were barred against Israelites, or Edom the only people by whom they were bidden to keep off them. Time was, and not so very long ago, when if Jews wanted to move along, they had to make their way by devious paths, so as not to be seen of men. For they dreaded the savage blow, or words and gestures of contempt which upon sensitive natures inflict a sharper wound than blows. And even to this day there are countries, some of them claiming to be great civilizers and world-rulers, where, as in the days of Deborah and Jael, so far as Jews are concerned, the high roads have become impossible and travellers have perforce to get on, if they are resolved to get on, by crooked by-paths.

Why, in the middle ages, that is to say up till about three or four hundred years ago, Jews were almost compelled to travel at night-time, so that no one could see them and ill-treat them. Thank God that things are altered in some countries at least ! The high road is here open to all, the high road to every honourable occupation.

And in quite a literal sense, too. Can you help thinking how great a thing it is that you live at a time when, and in a place where, you have been able to march, 100 strong and more, all Jewish lads, and not ashamed of it, but rather proud to be known as the Jewish Lads' Brigade—to march along the high road together from Spitalfields to Bayswater, not only unmolested, but protected, and—I hope I shall not make you conceited by saying so—even admired !

But do not imagine that the Brigade is a mere instrument for making you march up and down in a straight and orderly fashion, adorned with a kind of half-military accoutrements. It would take a wiser man than any I am acquainted with who should be able to calculate how far the effect will reach of such training as you are receiving. Even slight unconsidered acts of ours have consequences neither we nor any of us can foresee ; how much more then will those actions and movements, to which we accustom ourselves and deliberately cling. Things, as the saying is, hang together. It was a very wise man who said, " Sow an act, reap a habit ; sow a habit, reap a character ; sow a character, reap a destiny."

Let us look at some of the consequences that are likely to follow from the mere fact of your having joined the Jewish Lads' Brigade, and undertaken the duties connected therewith.

In the first place an institution like the Jewish Lads' Brigade is a sign that you are already part and parcel of the English nation, young as you are, and that you are preparing to take your share one day in the manhood of the land. When you march along the King's highway, you may have the delightful feeling that you are doing so not on sufferance, but by right—a right which you are earning by showing that you are taking the first steps to fit you for the defence of the safety and the honour of your country.

Our fathers, merely wishing to pass through Edom, were desirous to pay for whatever they got. But we have come to stay. We are then not only to take but to give. And where we receive so much, surely we ought also to give much. If we receive protection—the equal protection of the laws and power of England, we ought also to offer some of the strength of our youth and manhood. It is this spirit which the Jewish Lads'

Brigade helps to foster, where it already exists, and where it does not yet exist, to create.

But this is a long way off yet, though it is well to begin early to prepare for it. I once heard the Jewish boys of Whitechapel called " the wild boys of the East." If so, the best thing is to catch you young and tame you. A vast amount of good lies to hand for all of you who rightly use the opportunity the Brigade affords you. " *We* will march by the King's high way." This implies a marching together, a movement executed as one. None rushing on in front, nor straggling behind, but all submitting, restraining, impelling themselves for the advantage of all. A perfect battalion, I suppose, is that in which no one individual can be picked out as better or worse than the rest, and in which all are, as it were, moved by one spring, guided by one mind, impelled by one spirit. It is like a good choir where there is no attempt, unless the harmony demands it, for any person to sing louder than the rest, or to get even a fraction of a minute ahead of, or behind, the others ; it is like the choir of the Levites in Solomon's Temple (2 Chr. v. 13), of whom it is said, as a guide to choirs of all future generations that " the trumpeters and the choristers were as one, to make one sound to be heard in praising and thanking the Lord."

So the members of the Jewish Lads' Brigade must be as one. And this means that you must acquire a two-fold spirit. It means a spirit of movement and a spirit of rest. You must be ready as circumstances require to advance or to withdraw, to march and to camp. When the bugle sounds the advance, all must be ready to start. When you are ordered to stand at ease, you must all be ready to stand still. I am not sure that

the second thing isn't the harder of the two. I know
that you can march, steadily and without giving in. It
was a long and fatiguing march for you to-day, but you
all did it bravely, and not one of you fell out of the ranks.
But I was even more pleased by something else. You
were all drawn up in order waiting, patiently and for
rather a considerable time, outside the synagogue before
you came in. What a delightful thing it is that you
have already learned to march together and to rest together. May God give you the strength and the courage
to carry these lessons into your lives.

Yes, my young friends, throughout the whole of
our lives—while we are marching along the highway
of the King of kings on to the land of promise—it is
these two lessons we have to master : when we may have
to hasten, when we may have to slow down our pace ;
when to use the spur and when the reins.

In the first place then, your Brigade helps to cultivate
a sense of personal responsibility in you all. Each of
you knows, or ought to know, that the character, the
efficiency, the credit of the Brigade is in his keeping, and
so I trust you are led to strive your utmost for the glory
of the whole. Slovenliness, carelessness, listlessness,
idleness in any one tells on the rest.

You ought to have no room for dummy members.
Unfortunately there are in many societies, even in
religious Societies, even among Jews, members of this
class, who look like the rest and are called like the rest,
but who do nothing to justify their title.

In the old coaching days there was a four-horsed
coach that used to run along the great western road,
about which I have somewhere read a curious story.
On the box beside the driver there one day sat a gentle-

man who understood something about horses. As they were going along the gentleman said, " What is the matter with your off-leader ? " " Nothing's the matter with him." " But he doesn't pull a bit." " I know that." " Why did you harness him in then ? " " Well," said the coachman, " this is a four-in-hand, and master says, a four-in-hand must have four horses, never mind whether they pull or don't."

Now, you are a hundred-in-hand or thereabouts, but I hope that none of you will act on those lines and say : Whether I help the rest of the team along or not doesn't matter. I may be as slack as I like—it doesn't matter. It does matter very much to your companions, to your officers, but infinitely more it matters to you, for the very reason that you are not a horse but a human being, and that as your sense of responsibility to others becomes relaxed, so your whole character alters for the worse.

What a splendid lesson you are learning each of you to do his best for the good of the whole body. Depend upon it, dear boys, that the moment a youth does some strenuous action, without sparing himself, without thought of the gain to himself, but aiming at the honour of benefit of another, that moment he purges his soul of everything common and vulgar, and stamps himself of the true nobility of the human race.

Now, I told you that I was proud of you, that in your march none of you fell out. In another sense the Brigade teaches you not to " fall out." When Joseph sent his brethren to Canaan to fetch their and his father Jacob, he said to them : " See that ye fall not out by the way." Quarrelling and dissension destroy nations and communities. If the horses pull different ways the coach will be overturned. The Brigade teaches

you this lesson also.   All for one end, all for the one
cause, you must pull together.   I only hope that when
you are grown up, both as Jews and Englishmen, you
will pull together in a loving spirit like brothers.

Not the least important thing for you to learn is that
it may be sometimes necessary to repress oneself for the
good of the rest.   It is that, too, which all training like
yours helps you to acquire—the habit of obeying orders,
even the order to keep still, sometimes the most difficult
and the most trying in the world.   Officers engaged in
active service tell how hard it is to prevent young re-
cruits in their first battle from firing too early, and thus
spoiling the chance of victory.

What heroism is often involved in holding back, in
standing still, in simply, silently, bravely waiting.   It
is hardly possible to recall unmoved the story of what
occurred on the *Warren Hastings* which was wrecked
early last year off the Mauritius with hundreds of British
troops on board—all brought safely to land in the darkness and danger of that disastrous night.   But for the
perfection with which those men had learned to control
themselves, a panic would inevitably have seized upon
them all, and scarcely a life would have been saved.   But
the most pathetic and significant part of the story remains.   The officer who was told off to see that everybody was out of the vessel before quitting her himself,
called aloud from the deck as the ship was rapidly
filling : " Is there anybody else below ? " when a voice
was heard saying, " Please, sir, may I come up now ?
The water is getting rather high."   And so it was, for
on looking down through the hatchway, the officer perceived the man who had orders to remain below as
sentry, standing steadfast, immovable, up to his neck
in water, all the others having gone away.

There is little chance of such a thing occurring to any of you, for there is no naval counterpart of the Lads' Brigade at present, and the Brigade as such is never afloat ; but the principle just illustrated is the same whether on the ocean highway or on the King's highway, or on the high road of life, whether in battling with the waves or facing other foes, struggling with other difficulties. To learn how to restrain oneself, how to hold oneself in, is among the hardest, the most heroic of all the tasks of life. It is that which makes the difference not only between a mob and an army, but between the brute beast and the man, endowed by heaven above all other creatures with reason, will and conscience, and trying to perfect his life both by liberty and by law.

And lastly, let me ask a question of you. Do you not enjoy your hours spent in drilling and marching ? Of course you do ! I am told that most of you prefer it to all the games you ever play. And why ? Because this is a play for you, and more than a play. It is well that you should enjoy it, that it should be amusing, attractive, and interesting. But you will, dear boys, learn as you get older, that the greatest pleasures of life are just those pleasures that come by doing one's duty. And so you are also beginning to learn, as members of the Brigade, this great lesson of life. Doing one's duty is the greatest happiness. Duty and happiness are almost one and the same thing. May you all grow stronger and stronger in this desire to do your duty, and may you all win from duty done that happiness which is the blessed lot of those who put duty first and happiness second. Continue as you have begun by walking on the King's highway, and may the King of kings show you the highway unto Himself !

ON ASKING QUESTIONS

(*New West End Synagogue,*
October 1st, 1904.)

1 KINGS x. 1, 3 : " And when the Queen of Sheba heard of the fame of Solomon concerning the name of the Lord, she came to prove him with hard questions. And Solomon told her all her questions : there was not anything hid from the King, which he told her not."

IT must indeed have been a wonderful sight, that meeting of the Queen of Sheba with Solomon in all his glory. She had heard in her country, a long way off, of his greatness, and she came to do honour to him. But what most made her want to see him was the report of his wisdom.

In order to witness it for herself, to hear it from his own mouth, she did not mind all the trouble and expense of a long journey. She must have been herself a wise woman, for it is only the wise who value the wise properly. Fools are generally quite satisfied with their own cleverness ; if they were not self-satisfied they would not be fools. " The fool is wiser in his own conceit, than seven men that can give answer intelligently " (Proverbs xxvi. 16). The Bible uses " sluggard " in this last sentence where I have used " fool." But both mean the same. Fools think they know everything ; sluggards are too lazy to ask and so remain just as ignorant as if they were fools.

Solomon receives the Queen with great courtesy. She asks many questions, and hard ones, of him. With God's word and a wise and understanding heart to guide him, he is able to solve all her questions, and to give her instruction in many things. Many things are mentioned which she admires, his beautiful palace, his luxurious feasts, his armies of splendidly-apparelled servants, his cup-bearers, and the magnificent Temple. But most of all she is amazed at his wisdom. She is overcome with it all, " there was no more spirit in her " —as we should also say, " it took her breath away." For once, the reality was more than was expected.

And the effect of all that she heard and saw was that she herself was led to a belief in the God worshipped by King Solomon and his people Israel. " Blessed be the Lord, thy God," she exclaimed, " who delighted in thee, to set thee on the throne of Israel : because the Lord loved Israel for ever, and therefore He made thee King, to do judgment and justice."

What I want you to note is that all this came from asking questions. If she had never come and asked, she would probably never have known. Let me, then, say a few words about asking questions.

Every one who loves children loves them all the better for asking questions. It is a sign that you are thinking, and unless you think, you cannot learn. It is a sign that you are not always going to remain a child, but will in due time become a man or woman. And no sensible person will think any the worse of you if you ask questions about things which are hard to understand and which you cannot make out for yourselves. There is no disgrace in not knowing ; we are born ignorant ; the disgrace is in not wanting or caring to know.

Now, there are many kinds of questions—good and bad, wise and silly, kind and cruel. Not all are like those which the Queen of Sheba asked of Solomon. She came to him because of his fame for what he had done for the glory of God—and she learned much from him, which made her happy. We know of at least one question which far from leading to happiness led to the loss of it. " Did God indeed say you shall not eat of the tree ? " That was the serpent's question, and it led to Eve's disobedience, and caused unhappiness. So, you see, much depends on the spirit in which questions are asked.

There are certain kinds of questions you ought to be on your guard against. Nothing is more painful than to hear children, in reply to every order given them by those in authority over them, ask—But why shall I do this ? Why not that ? You must learn to suppress such questions as that. You have very often to obey orders, not to ask *why* the orders are given. If a soldier waited till he knew the exact motive for every command he would lose the battle. A battle covers a great deal of ground, and only the commander-in-chief knows the whole plan. Each soldier cannot know the whole plan, and so must obey without question.

> Theirs not to reason why ;
> Theirs but to do and die.

Even to die if necessary in the performance of their duty.

Some people ask questions, not because they want to know more than they do know, but because they want to show how clever they are. I hope you will never be like them ; especially not at school, because it would be a dreadful thing if Jewish boys and girls got a name for being forward, or pert, or conceited.

Then, some boys and girls ask questions to waste time. They try to get their teachers off the subject by asking about all sorts of irrelevant things. Or they ask the first thing that comes into their mind, they cannot keep their attention to the thing in hand, but must ask and ask. The worst thing about this kind of question is that the asker does not even wait for the answer. Before his first question is answered he is ready with another question. Now, that is rather rude. One thing you must really learn : it is that if you *do* ask a question, wait for the answer and try to remember it.

Sometimes a question is itself as good as an answer. It makes you think out the answer for yourself. Good teachers always question children in that way. One of the wisest men that ever lived, Socrates, did nearly all his teaching in that way ; he used to ask his pupils— and they were grown-up people—question after question, until it seemed to them that they themselves got at the truth, and in that way it was impressed upon them much more lastingly. There is an old legend that Abraham, when he was a boy, often taught wisdom to people much older than himself simply by asking them questions. For instance, here is one of the stories they tell about him. Abraham's father, Terah, was, it is said, a maker and seller of idols ; and Abraham was sometimes left at home to take care of the shop. One day an old man came in and selected an idol he wanted to buy. Abraham took it down from the shelf, handed the image to the purchaser, and received the price for it. Then as the man turned to leave, he said to him :

" How old are you, sir ? "   " Seventy years."   " And
how old do you think this idol is ? "   He did not know.
" It was made yesterday," said Abraham, and he went
on :   " How can you, who were born seventy years ago,
worship a god which is no more than a day old ? "   The
man saw the force of the question, thought a moment,
gave back the image, received his money again, and
departed made wiser by a couple of sensible questions.

But we must guard ourselves against asking foolish
questions, or questions that we could answer ourselves
if we only took a little trouble.   It would be a very
bad thing for us if we always got other people to do
our thinking for us.

Once upon a time there was a King who was a very
thoughtful man.   He thought to himself—There are
only three things I want to know ; if I know them I
shall never make a mistake.   What is the most important time for every action ? who are the most important
people with whom I am to concern myself ? and what is
the most important action I can do to them ?   So he
announced throughout his Kingdom that whoever would
tell him these things—the best time, the most suitable
person, the most important work—should be richly
rewarded.

He soon received all sorts of answers that did not
agree with one another.   Some said—To know the
right time for doing everything you must draw up before-
hand a list of things to be done every day, month and
year.   Others said—It's no use drawing things up before-
hand.   You must wait and watch, and then ask more
wise men if that's the right time.   As to the most
important persons, some said they were the soldiers,
ministers of State, who help to rule, some that they were

the lawyers, and others that they were the clergymen. Then what is the most important work ? Some said learning, some fighting, some praying. All this only confused the poor King.

Now there happened to be living in a wood some way from his capital a hermit, who had a name for being a very wise man ; but he had little to do with kings, and only common people went to see him. The King resolved to go and ask him these questions. So he dressed himself in simple clothes, and before reaching the hermit's hut, he got off his horse, told his bodyguard to keep at a distance and wait for him, while he went alone to the hermit. He was an old man and feeble, but was working hard, digging his garden. The King went up to him, and told him what he had come for—to learn from him the right time, person, action, so that he might have no reason ever to regret missing them. The hermit listened to the King, but answered not a word ; he only went on working—exhausted though he was. The King thereupon took the spade from the hermit and began digging, and when he had been at work for some hours, until he was tired, handed the spade back. " You have not answered my questions," said the King. " There comes somebody running," said the hermit. The King turned and saw a bearded, wild-looking man ; he ran with his hand on his side, and as he rushed up fell down in a swoon. It was soon seen that the man was severely wounded. The King, with the hermit, staunched the blood, cleansed the wound and bound it up, and placed the stranger on a couch. Night came on and the King, exhausted, fell asleep, near the stranger. Early in the morning the wounded

S.C.   P man awoke, and fixing his eyes upon the King exclaimed, "Pardon!" "I have nothing to pardon thee for, I do not even know thee." "Thou knowest not me, but I know thee. Know then that I am thy enemy. I heard of thy coming here alone, and I came and hid myself to slay thee. But as thou didst delay here with the hermit, I grew impatient, and quitting my hiding-place thy soldiers found me and wounded me. And now thou hast saved my life, thou whose life I had sworn to take. Pardon, O King, and let me be to the end of thy days thy devoted slave." The King readily pardoned him, and was delighted to have so easily made a friend of his enemy, and sent for his own physician and gave orders to his bodyguard to treat the man with every kindness.

And now, as he was about to leave, he said to the hermit, "For the last time I ask thee, wilt thou give me no answer to my questions?"

"They are already answered." "Answered? How so?" "Why plainly. If yesterday thou hadst not pitied my weakness, and helped me to dig this garden, but hadst returned alone, that fine fellow would have attacked and perchance have slain thee. Consequently the right time was when thou tookest the spade from my hand, and I was the most important person, and the most important work was to do me a service. Then when the other ran up, the most important time was when thou wast tending him, for if thou hadst not dressed his wound he would have died without being reconciled with thee. Therefore the most important person was he, and that which thou didst unto him was the most important act. Thus, remember, that the most important time is always one, *now*; it is the most important because only the present moment is really ours ; and the most important man is the one with whom at each present moment we are in touch ; and the most important work is to do good to him." Thus relates Tolstoy in *King Assarhardon.*.

It is sometimes not only permissible, but obligatory, to ask questions. On the Passover eve, you will remember, it is your duty as children to ask questions, and it is the delight of your parents to answer you. They rejoice to see you take interest in your religion, and they are never more pleased than when you ask them sensible questions about the synagogue service, the home ceremonies, the Bible, and the stories which it tells and the wonderful lessons it teaches. You must try to understand these things, and you cannot understand them at all unless you ask for explanations. You must not ask so as to trip up your father and mother, just to puzzle them and worry them. But ask so that you may understand. If they use a word you do not know the meaning of, then do not let it pass. If they tell you things you cannot understand, tell them so, and they will try to make it simple and clear for you.

Of course, you must not expect to get a satisfactory answer to *all* the questions you can ask. For—and this is my last point to-day—I want you to remember that there are questions which cannot be answered. Yes we have all of us to learn to wait. There are things you cannot understand while you are children, and you must be content to wait many years until you are grown up, and your understanding has grown with your body. Sensible parents and teachers often have to say to children who ask questions, Wait till you are older, and then you will be able to understand.

And good and sensible children will be content to wait ; they will trust those who love them, and who for their children's good sometimes put them off with " by and by things will be clearer."

And some things there are we shall never be able quite to understand while we are in this life. Probably God did not want us to understand them, or He would have told us. A few minutes ago we were offering up prayers for those of our dear ones who have died. People ask, Why did they die, many of them very early in life, many of them were so good and kind and true ; and were so much wanted. And what *is* death ? And why was it sent into the world ? And to all these questions all that the wise men can do is only to give part of an answer, which is very often no answer at all. No, Solomon himself, with all his wisdom, could not answer these questions. This only we know—that He who sent us death is the same God who gave us life ; that nothing but what is good can come from Him. So we must trust Him without questioning Him ; trust Him with our hearts, even when we cannot understand. And, my dear children, in this trust and faith may you grow up !

LOVE COVERETH ALL SINS

(*New West End Synagogue,
Passover, April 20th,* 1900.)

PROVERBS x. 12 : "Love covereth all sins."

Do you know what is the easiest thing in all the world ? I have heard people say the easiest thing in all the world is doing nothing. I doubt it. No work is often the hardest work. How tired you get of it, for instance, in the holidays, and how glad you are, let alone your mothers and fathers, when the holidays are over.

Then I have known people say the easiest thing in all the world is spending money. There is something in that. People who have money find it easy enough to spend, though to spend it sensibly—well, that's not easy.

No, the easiest thing in all the world is to find out other people's faults. Haven't you noticed how quickly we can see them, how much more quickly than our own, though our own are much nearer to us than other people's ?

But though it may be the easiest or one of the easiest things in the world, surely it is not the best, it is not the noblest, it is not the holiest thing, this of seeing other people's faults and fastening on them and making much of them, and condemning them. There is something far worthier of us, and what that is is expressed

in the words I started with from Proverbs : " Love
covereth all sins."

What is the meaning of " Love covereth all sins ? "
It may mean this—Love covers all sins in the one who
loves. Because a person loves, his sins are put out of
sight and are forgiven. If a child is of a loving and
affectionate nature, though he may have all sorts of
faults and may have done all sorts of wrong even, parents
say of him, Well he *is* such an affectionate little fellow,
one *must* forgive him. There is no doubt that in families,
at all events, love leads to forgiveness.

But there is another meaning also—Love covereth
all sins in another. If a person has real love in his
heart it leads him to cover up, to hide, to overlook, to
forgive the sins of another. It is only a bitter, sour
heart that takes pleasure in finding out and showing
up the faults of others, even it may be of their own
friends and relations. It is a sweet and loving nature
that covers these faults over, that says, " Well, I don't
want to hear evil of those whom I love," and if he has
heard it, says, " I do not suppose I know all about
how it really happened. How should I ? God knows ;
God alone knows all ; He alone can judge."

I think this last is the true meaning, though, if you
like it you are welcome to remember both.

Now I do not for a moment say that whatever evil
you see done, you are to take no notice of it and let it
work out any mischief it can. God holds us answerable
for one another, and the wrong which we could prevent
being done, or the sin which we could persuade another
to give up, even a young brother or sister, or schoolboy
or schoolgirl friend, and about which we take no sort
of trouble, we shall one day ourselves have to answer

for. But when we speak of evil in another, it is our duty to question ourselves very closely, and ask : For what reason do I do it ? Is it because I want to do him any good ? Is it because I love him ? Or is it because I dislike him and I want him to be thought badly of ? And is it that I hope that the worse another appears the better I shall seem to be ? Our hearts deceive us often very much in these matters, and we slip into this sin of talking against one another so easily that it is well to remember that no fault-finding ever does any good unless it springs from love, and is guided by love.

A man who had tried to train himself to a life of holiness once received a precious lesson. " It was my custom in my youth," he said, " to rise at night from my sleep, to watch, pray and read the Koran, (or holy book of the followers of Mohammed). One night as I was thus engaged, my father, a good and godly man of practised virtue, awoke. My brothers continued in their sleep. ' Behold,' said I to my father, ' thy other children are lost in slumbers, giving no thought to God, while I alone wake to praise Him.' ' Son of my soul,' said he, ' it is better to sleep than to wake to mark the faults of thy brothers.' "

Yês, true love covereth all sins in another by helping him to get rid of them Such was the love of Moses for Israel. How he must have been tried by the people he did so much to help, to save, to bless. True, now and then, very rarely indeed he lost patience with them —two or three times at most in eighty years, during which he had dealings with them—but even those moments of complaining soon passed, and taking his life as a whole it was one long covering of his people's sins. Why ? I know no other reason than this : it was because he loved them. I do not see how he could have borne otherwise with their constant grumblings, and fretfulness, and faithlessness.

What have we read this morning ? The people blame him for taking them out of Egypt. " What is this thou hast done unto us. Thou wantest us to die here in the wilderness. Let us alone and we will serve the Egyptians." How tenderly he deals with them. Moses makes no answer of harsh rebuke, such as he might think they deserve. His reply is : " Stand still and see the salvation of the Lord." His love covers their transgression. They cross the sea and are safe. Once more they murmur against Moses on account of the bitter waters they are to drink. But love sweetens the bitterest draft. A little later they are guilty of the greatest sin against God and exchange Him for an idol of gold ; but Moses would cover their transgression. He pleads for them, he prays for them, he offers to lay down his own life for them, if perchance that might save them, and if by such love he could cover his people's sin.

I fancy I hear some of you say—Well now, you tell us love covers all sins. But oughtn't one to speak the truth—and if it be true that a person has sinned shouldn't we tell the truth, however dreadful it may sound ? Or is love to cover not only other people's sins, but the truth about them as well ?

Well, dear children, if any of you feel like that I can only say I am very glad you are so passionately fond of the truth about other people, and I only hope you will be always equally fond of it when it has something to do with yourselves. But let me remind you of what I am sure you have already been taught, that while everything you say should be true, not everything that is true ought to be said. Many a truth need not be said—and many had better not be said. You are not bound to tell all the world about the last scrape your brother got into. Most unkind things there is no call at all to say. And, besides, it is quite possible to combine truth with charity. A really good man or woman never separates them. Let me explain this by an illustration.

There is a story told about Alexander the Great, King of Macedon. An eminent painter was asked to paint Alexander's portrait. He was told he was to give a noble portrait of the King, as perfect a likeness as possible, so that everybody should know him at sight. Well, the artist found himself in a great difficulty. Alexander in one of his wars had been struck by a sword, and across his forehead there was left a big scar. The painter said to himself, What am I to do ? If I put the scar on the King's brow into my picture, people will say it disfigures the monarch, and his admirers will be offended ; if I leave it out it will not be a perfect likeness. What do you think he did ? He hit upon a happy way out of the difficulty. He painted the Emperor leaning on his elbow, with his forefinger on his forehead, like a man in thought, his finger quite accidentally, as it seemed, covering the scar.

Might not we do something of the same kind, and when we describe or speak about people, without saying a word about them that is untrue, let the finger of charity cover their faults ? Depend upon it that without such love and charity we shall go astray in the world, and make such mistakes as shall sooner or later put us to the blush. The people who trust to their wits alone are not always wisest.

In one of Wordsworth's poems —I hope you will find time to read some of that poet's writings, if you haven't done so already—he tells a story how he came to name a certain promontory that juts out into a certain lake. It was harvest time, and the poet and a couple of friends were walking about near the lake watching the reapers at their work. Suddenly they caught sight at the brink of the lake of a peasant dressed in peasant's garb, fishing. They were greatly shocked that a poor man should be idling his time away in angling, at the very season when every moment was precious in the harvest field. Reckless, thoughtless person, they said, not to be reaping now like the rest and laying in store for the winter. They blamed him for a lazy fellow. While they were talking against him he turned round, and then they saw—they saw and understood—they saw a man worn down by sickness, gaunt and lean, with sunken cheeks and wasted limbs. He was too feeble for labour in the field, he was only fit to stand all day and fish with rod and line, and for such a man he surely was not idle. Then the poet tells how ashamed these gentry were who were lounging about at their leisure ; they all made themselves reproaches for having thought so unkindly of another. They saw—

> What need there is to be reserved in speech,
> And temper all our thoughts with charity.

That place they named Point Rash Judgment. We all, dear children, at some time, and perhaps more than once, reach Point Rash Judgment. But we can avoid it for our own comfort and to the blessings of others, if we notice the caution which our wise men have set up, before we get to Point Rash Judgment, and which says on one side, " Judge not another until thou art in his place," and on the other, " Judge all men charitably."

One day we shall ourselves need to be kindly and mercifully judged—yes, the very best of us when we come before Him in whose eyes the angels are not pure. But if we have been gentle and tender to others, if we have not been too hard upon those who have erred out of the right path, but rather have stretched out a hand to help them back, and have strengthened them both by our words and our example ; if we have forgiven those who have offended against us, and not shut our heart even to those who have smitten it, the God of Love will open wide His arms to us, however faulty we may have been in other ways, and will say : My love suffices to cover all your transgressions.

SILENCE AND SPEECH

*(Central Synagogue,
November 19th, 1898.)*

ECCLESIASTES iii. 7 : " There is a time to be silent, and a time
to speak."

HAVE you ever thought what a marvellous gift this is
of speech ?   That by merely moving our tongue and
mouth we can thus make each other understand whatever we think or remember or feel ; whatever we fear
or hope ; that by means of language the ignorant can
be instructed and all the knowledge of all the wise men
of the world can be handed on to other people—for
you know, of course, that all books are language,
with signs in place of sounds ; that by means of
speech we can persuade people to do what otherwise
they would not, and dissuade them from doing what
otherwise they would do, that, in fact, we can by this
gift of speech carry on with success all the affairs of our
daily life—is it not a wonderful thing ?   Can we be
grateful enough for it ?   Think of the state of those poor
children, who are speechless themselves and to whom
the whole world is speechless, how great and sad their
privation, so that everybody pities them—and say,
ought not you to be deeply grateful that you have been
enriched with that wondrous power of speech ?

But all God's gifts must be made a wise use of, or

else they are spoilt, and do harm instead of good to us and to others. Some of you might perhaps say, Well, since I've got the power of speech, I will not fail to make abundant use of it. How delighted my parents must be to know that I am not dumb! I think I will let all the world know it too. This is just the error which the wise man wanted to check when he said, " Every thing is beautiful in its season." " There is a time to be silent as well as a time to speak."

Certainly God intended us to be very cautious how we use our tongue. First, He never meant us to use it as much as our eyes and ears. For we have two ears and two eyes, and only one tongue, and if we had been meant to talk as much as we hear and see, we should have had two or perhaps four tongues. Also notice another thing, which the Jewish teachers of old have drawn our attention to, that Nature has double guarded our tongue. First there is a wall of flesh—our lips, and then there is a wall of bone—teeth, and then only you get to the tongue. Yet somehow or other the tongue is such an unruly member of the body that it breaks through both walls, and often does more mischief than we can remedy with all the rest of our strength.

One of the most difficult things in the world it is to know when to be silent, when to leave off speaking. Many a beautiful speech has been spoilt by the speaker saying just a little too much. If you have been speaking, isn't it nicer to leave off and let people say, " Well, I should like to hear that young gentleman or lady say a little more," than, " I could have done with a good deal less." There was a great Greek philosopher to whom a vain young person once came to learn from him the art of speaking. The young man talked such an

immense quantity, that the philosopher had to stop him
and said, " I shall be glad to be your instructor, but I
shall have to charge you double my usual fee." "Why?"
" You see I have to teach you not only how to speak,
but how to be silent."

" There is a time to be silent." To you, my young
friends, I should say, it is especially then when you
have received the commands of those who love you
and have authority over you—of parents and teachers.
There is no better test of a true-hearted and a well-bred
child than that of willing, unquestioning obedience. I
fear there is a great deal too much of argument and
self-assertion among some of our young people. They
are so much cleverer in their own esteem than their
elders, that they do not know that no one will ever be
fitted to command others who has not learnt to obey.
To do a parent's bidding after having argued against
it, asked for reasons why it should be obeyed, spoils
it of every charm. And children should not always
protest even if they are being a little unjustly treated
by their elders. Suppose your teacher thinks *you*
spoke when it was your neighbour, you need not be
too loud in protesting that it wasn't you. In life many
of us have to endure misunderstandings and suspicions
of this kind, and it is good training to you when young
to learn to bear such things silently.

And this leads to another answer to the question:
When is the time to be silent ? When we feel that we
are getting angry or losing our temper, and we are
about to say sharp and unkind things, which are sure
to wound, because we wish them to wound. I have
heard of children who, as they say, were ready to bite
their tongue off after they had said a hasty or a cruel

word, but biting the tongue off won't cure the wound. If a sword has once pierced a person's heart, it is not much good to break the sword. Sometimes there comes over children a strange feeling—they call it " feeling horrid." Never speak when you feel horrid, for what you say will probably be much more horrid than you feel.

There is a time to be silent. When ? When we feel ourselves thinking ill of another, and we are going to spread all the ill we know or imagine ; then is the time to put a restraint upon our tongues and bid them be silent. The unspoken word is ours ; the word once spoken is ours no longer, and no power on earth can recall it. It is swifter than the lightning, and it dodges us about in all directions, so that we never can come up with it. There was once a woman who fell out with a friend of hers, and believing then all sorts of dreadful things about her, she told them right and left to all whom she met. But when her anger had cooled and she looked into the matter she found that what she believed true was not true at all. Well, she was not exactly a bad-hearted person—in fact, her heart was better than her tongue, and she began to feel very, very sorry. So she went to a Rabbi and told him all she had done and begged of him to tell her what she should do to make it good. " Go," said the Rabbi, " to the market place, buy a fowl and take it home, and as you go along—you live about half an hour from the market, don't you ?—pluck the feathers from the fowl one by one and let them fall on the ground, so that by the time you reach home the bird may be well plucked." She did as she was told, and as she went along her path was marked by a stream of bird's feathers floating and flying along the road. Presently she came back to the clergyman, delighted with herself and with the good man who had given her no heavier penance, and said with great glee : " Sir, I have done exactly as you told me —here's the bird, you see it hasn't got a feather left on." " My good woman," said the Rabbi, " don't congratulate yourself in such a hurry ; you have only done half your task. Now go and pick all the feathers up again, and bring them to me." Off trudged the woman, but in the meantime the wind had blown the feathers in all directions, and after hours of searching she could only get together a few miserable feathers that wouldn't have been enough to cover a sparrow. " Oh, sir," she cried, " I looked everywhere and ever so long, but, alas ! they are all blown away." " Now," said the Rabbi, " let this be a lesson to you. Your words lightly spoken fly about like those feathers so easily, so airily ; but to gather them together again is what neither you nor any living being is able to do." Ah, if you will only remember the wise man's counsel—" There's a time to be silent," and if you will only think that the time to be silent is just when you want to say the most cruel things about other people—what a lot of undeserved pain you would spare them, and what a lot of deserved pain you might save yourselves !

But you will say—Am I only to be silent ? Heaven forbid. You were never intended to spend your days in silence. Among some of our neighbours they have whole communities living in monasteries, and spending days and days without speaking a word. There is a well-known brotherhood in France, where the monks live in their separate cells, and where they never speak to one another more than once a week. And there is even a silent sisterhood—a whole institution of ladies who do their work year in year out without saying a word to each other. I dare say these people mean well ; and probably they don't fall out quite so much and so often ; but I don't believe they please God a bit by constantly holding their tongues. Man was created a speaking animal : that was one of the great differences between man and the brute. The first intelligent act that is recorded of Adam is that he gave names to all living things.

There is, therefore, a time to speak. Those who love you love you all the more for your lively, childlike talk. To parents there is no music like the merry sound of children's voices ; you yourselves, when you grow older and wiser, you will wonder what it was they found so interesting in your prattle—but then none but a parent can have a parent's joy in these things.

No one would stop you when you speak, nor when you speak in eagerness to know more, nor if you would unburden your hearts to those who can understand you and feel for you in all the little troubles that find their way even into a child's life.

" There is a time to speak." When *you* are asked questions, you must answer if you can. If you are called, answer at once. Some children are silent just when they ought to speak. They let their mother or nurse call again and again and pay no attention. They hear but they do not speak. And so at school. You often have to be silent there. But often you are expected to speak. When it is your turn to recite or to read from the book, do your best. Speak as clearly as you can ; sound the words nicely and with proper expression. Do not repeat it in a monotonous, careless way, as though it did not interest you. Be eager and ready to speak when it is your turn and time to do it. " The world exists by means of the voices of the children in school," said a Rabbi. He meant that when you are full of life at your lessons, when you enjoy them, when your voices are merry and cheerful as you answer what you are asked, then the world is safe at least for another generation.

And then another time to make your voice heard is during worship in the synagogue, while the Psalms are being sung. I do wish some of you wouldn't be so bashful about joining in the singing here. You must not imagine that you are excused singing God's praises because a choir is provided in the synagogue. They cannot take your place ; they are only intended to lead you. You ought to feel as unsatisfied if I were to pray for you and instead of you, as you would be if I were to breakfast and dine for you. On Saturday last, I was in a small synagogue where there is no choir, but where every member of the congregation joined in the service and where especially the voices of children could be heard, all keeping in time and tune, so that it was quite delightful. You could do the same very easily, if you would get your mothers to obtain the music for you and some one who can play would go over the music with you on the piano. Then, when the time comes in Synagogue for singing it would be a time for you also to join, and would not be, as too many make it, a time to be silent.

Among the Sephardim, that is to say the ancient congregation whose chief synagogue is in Bevis Marks, there is an excellent custom. The little boys read aloud the lesson from the Prophets — the *Haphtarah*—

the boys do it very often instead of grown-up people. I know a little boy who did it when he was only eight years old. This is a fine thing. Of course it is not easy to learn enough Hebrew to understand the Prophets ; and, equally of course, no one ought to recite what he does not understand. But how excellent it is when boys *do* know and understand enough to perform this service for the congregation ! Then is fulfilled the words of the eighth Psalm : " Out of the mouth of babes and sucklings hast Thou established strength."

In the Sabbath Psalm it is said : " It is a good thing to give thanks unto the Lord, and to sing praises unto Thy name, O most High ! To show forth Thy loving-kindness in the morning, and Thy faithfulness every night ; with an instrument of ten strings." In the last words the reference is to a harp or lyre. But, as has been well said, every child is an instrument of ten strings. You have two eyes to look to God, two ears to listen to His word, two hands to work for Him, two feet to go on His errands—that makes eight. And you have a heart to prompt and stir you to praise Him, and a tongue to utter His praise. May each of you be such an instrument, increasing in melody and compass as you grow older. But even now, while you are young, may you take your part in the world's chorus of praise; and may your hearts and tongues always be in tune. And now rise and repeat after me : Almighty God ! we thank Thee for all Thy gifts to us for this holy day of rest, and for the lessons we learn on it : lessons of Thy goodness and of our duty.

Especially we thank Thee for the gift of speech which Thou hast granted us. Without it how dull our life would be. With it, thanks to Thy loving-kindness, mind can speak to mind and heart to heart. May we never make an evil use of our speech, never use it to deceive, or to lie; never to say unkind things to one another, or of one another; never to speak sinful and unholy words. Help us to love the truth, to speak it, even though we may sometimes suffer for it.

But above all help me to use my speech to tell Thee all I feel, and all I want, and to thank Thee for Thy Fatherly and never-ending love to me and mine.

"Lord open Thou my lips, and my mouth shall declare Thy praise."

THE NEW YEAR

*(Sermon for the first day of New Year, 1898,
For the Children's Services, organized by the United Synagogue.)*

MY DEAR CHILDREN,—I want to tell you how welcome
you are, all of you, who have come here to-day to begin
the New Year in earnest prayer to God Almighty. You
know that all the synagogues are full to-day; they are
crowded with people who feel something in their hearts
that forces them into God's House; they are so full
that there is not room in them for you boys and girls.

Fortunately you have friends who love you and think
for you (though you may not know them), and they
have taken care that you too shall be able to worship
together on these most solemn days of the whole year,
and get from them many of the blessings they offer
to the faithful children of Israel. It is a glorious and
a happy thing to know—is it not?—that we are all
of us, young and old, praying in ever so many places
on these holy days to the God of Israel, and praying
almost at the same moment the very same words which
our fathers and mothers have prayed for a thousand
years and more when they kept their New Years. For
this, dear children, so far as you are concerned, you
have to thank your friends of the United Synagogue.

I would ask you to do your utmost, by your thoughtful
and respectful behaviour, as well as by devoutly joining

in the prayers, to prove that the services held here are not only services *for* children, but—what is more important and dearer to God, and to all who truly love you—services *by* children. And may God incline His ear when you raise your voices and your hearts to Him, and help you to-day and every day to become worthy of His loving-kindness !

How are you going to begin the New Year which God, in His goodness, has given you ? Is there anything God would like you to take with you into the New Year and keep to even the end of it ? These questions may be answered by a few words that are to be found in the Book of Joshua, chapter i, verse 9.

" Have not I commanded thee ? Be strong and of a good courage ; be not afraid, neither be thou dismayed : for the Lord thy God is with thee whithersoever thou goest."

God is speaking these words to Joshua, the servant of Moses, who succeeded his master in the leadership of the people of Israel. Joshua was about to undertake a very solemn and difficult task. He was to guide his people into a new country. He and his people were to lead a life in many ways quite different from that to which they had been accustomed. They were going to exchange a life in the wilderness for one in a settled land. And they were going to meet with many difficulties, and would have to fight many and strong enemies ; and, if they had to depend upon themselves alone, there was not a soul among them who could say how it would all end. Everything about the future was dark and unknown, and might well seem, to mortal men, full of danger. Perhaps Joshua was a little anxious. Then God said to him, " Be strong and of

good courage "—once, twice, thrice He said it. " Have
not I commanded thee ? Be strong and of a good
courage ; be not afraid, neither be thou dismayed ;
for the Lord thy God is with thee whithersoever thou
goest."

Now, a New Year is as unknown as a new country—
and more so. Joshua and Caleb had got some little
acquaintance with the land of Canaan while they were
spying it out, though the rest of the people knew nothing
about it for themselves. But no one has been into the
New Year to find out what it will be like, and to tell us
concerning it. It is as if a thick curtain were hanging
in front of it ; we cannot see a month, a week, a day
before us, no, not an hour, or a minute.

And not only do we not know what the New Year
has in store for us, but it seems that God does not want
us to know. There is a story told in the Midrash of a
little boy who was walking along the road carrying
a vessel that was carefully covered. A traveller going
along the same way noticed the boy and what he was
carrying, and said to him, " My child, what is in that
vessel ? " " If," answered the child—he was a witty
little fellow—" if my father had wanted all the world
to know what was in the vessel, he would not have
ordered me to keep it closely covered." So is it with
the New Year. If God had wanted us to know what
the New Year will bring us, He would not have hung
so thick a veil in front of it that no one can see the
least distance beyond the present moment. Yes, dear
children, what the New Year will bring us not a soul
on earth can tell,—whether health or sickness, good
fortune or evil fortune, happiness or misery, life or
death.

But while we do not know and cannot hope to know what the New Year may bring to us, we do know what we ought to bring *to it* : *courage and a brave heart, first* in trusting God, and *next* in doing our duty. " Have I not commanded thee ? Be strong and of good courage : for the Lord thy God is with thee whithersoever thou goest."

First, then, we have to be strong and of good courage in believing and trusting in God. He is with us whithersoever we go—by land and by sea, sleeping and waking, in the light and in the darkness. There was once a boy who was being asked questions about God. " Tell me," said the gentleman who was questioning him, " where God is, and I will give you an orange." " Tell me," said the boy, " where God is not, and I will give you two oranges." Do you remember the beautiful words of the 139th Psalm ? " Whither can I go from Thy spirit ? or whither can I flee from Thy presence ? If I ascend into heaven, Thou art there ; if I make the grave my bed, behold Thou art there. If I take the wings of the morning " (that is, If I could fly as fast and as far as the rays of the rising sun), " or if I were to make my dwelling in the uttermost parts of the sea, even there shall Thy hand lead me and Thy right hand shall hold me." Where, indeed, is God not ? And in the New Year also God will surely be with you. He will be with you and your parents and all whom you love. Ah ! dear children, if we did not go forth into the New Year with trust in God, knowing that wherever we go, whatever may befall us, however weak and helpless we may be in ourselves, God will be by our side, and on our side, well might we tremble to live a single day, let alone a whole year, or a long life. If God were not

with us, who could make us feel strong and of good
courage ? If God *is* with us, who can make us afraid ?

On the coast of Brittany there live a people, brave,
hardy and pious, sea-faring and fishing folk. Whenever they pushed forth from their harbours into the
deep they used, it is said, to pray this simple prayer
(some of them perhaps do so still) : " Good Lord,
remember me ! Thy sea is so large, and my boat is so
small. Good Lord, remember me ! " Verily, dear
children, we are but a speck in God's creation, and our
life is but an instant next to His who lives for ever and
ever. Might not each of us, young and old, say, " The
vessel of my life is so small, the ocean of Thy world is
so large. Good Lord, remember me."

And no sincere prayer of this kind is ever offered up
in vain. To those who truly and fervently pray to
God to remember them, especially to remember them
to-day, on this holy Day of Remembrance, to them
an answer will certainly be given. Because they have
the strength and the courage to trust God, *more* strength
and courage is given them for the time to come (that is
God's way of dealing with His children), and they will
hear God's voice in the depth of their own hearts, saying
to them, " Be not afraid, be not dismayed, for I am
with thee whithersoever thou goest."

But besides being strong and courageous in trusting
to God, whatever the New Year may bring with it, we
need to be strong and courageous in doing the duties
which another year of life brings for every one of us.
A New Year is a great gift of God to us all. I doubt
whether we think as much of it as we should. But
if a whole year is an important thing for any one, it is
especially important to a young boy or girl. When

people have lived sixty or seventy years, time flies
with them, and one year passes, they tell us, very much
like another. But with you every new year marks a
great and distinct change. Your bodies are growing ;
your minds also, I hope, are growing ; new desires
come into your hearts ; your characters are changing ;
you are leaving your childhood a long way behind you,
and passing through youth swiftly on to man- and
womanhood. It is like going into a new and unexplored
country. It may all look very pleasant and delightful
at a distance ; but all sorts of difficulties and dangers
may be awaiting you there, not ordinary difficulties
and dangers, but difficulties in keeping to what you
have been taught and know to be right and true, as well
as dangers to the life and health of that soul which
God has given you as a token of His greatest love for
you.

How, then, should you try to enter upon the New
Year ? By being, as God also said to Joshua, " strong
and very courageous, to observe to do according to
all the Law which Moses My servant commanded thee."
To do right as God has ordered it, to fight against our
own inclination to transgress His commands, often
requires greater strength and courage than to meet
and overcome a mighty human foe. Yet in these
things also God will be with you. If you have the real
longing within you to be good Jews and Jewesses,
faithful followers of the Law of Moses, God will assuredly
be with you whithersoever you go.

Be strong then and of good courage in the resolutions
you form to-day. God will help you to finish what you
worthily begin. Resolve that from to-day you will strive
to get rid of many of your childish faults, that you will

prepare yourselves for a life of true manliness or woman-liness. Resolve that during the coming year you will never stoop to tell a lie, nor to act one, no, not even if it gets you great gain, not even if it helps to get you off a hard punishment. Be firmly determined never to do or say either an unjust thing, or a cruel thing, or a mean thing, or an impure thing. Make up your minds to struggle bravely against indolence and sloth— two of the worst enemies a young boy or girl has to contend with—and resolve to do with all your might whatever good thing your hand finds to do, whether at school, or at home, or in your trade or business. For all these things no little strength and courage are needed.

Be brave especially to resist an evil example. " If sinners entice thee, consent thou not." You are old enough, even the youngest here, to know good from evil, and you must bear well and constantly in mind that the example of others, boys or girls, or even grown up men and women, can never make wrong right, or right wrong. God has settled those matters for us in His Word, and the example of others cannot alter them. Be firm and resolved therefore to be true to the Faith in which you have been born and brought up ; to honour the Sabbath and holy days of the Lord ; not to defile yourselves by food He has forbidden, and never to omit your daily thanks and prayers to Him who has preserved you unto this day, and will not fail to take loving care of you in the coming time.

Be strong and brave to confess where you have erred. It is only weak and cowardly people who think they can't afford to admit they have been wrong and have done wrong. Go over now in your own hearts as much of your doings in the old year as you can recall, and ask yourselves whether you have been all that you should have been during the past year, in your own homes to your mothers and fathers, to your sisters and brothers ; and if your hearts tell you you have not, why resolve to-day that you will be more gentle and kind and loving to one another at home, that you will spare your parents every grief and vexation, that they shall never have reason to complain of you and say, " Our love and care have been thrown away upon a thankless child," but rather that they shall have reason to bless you and say, " This child shall comfort us for our work and for the toil of our hands."

Such are the promises and the duties this New Year asks of you. Do not, I entreat you, put them off for another year. Who knows whether you will be in life another year to make and fulfil resolutions like these, and, even if you are, who knows whether the same opportunities will be yours, whether God may not have taken from you and have taken to Himself some of those to whom you owed so much, and to whom you made so poor a return for all their love to you.

Of course it may happen to you, as it has happened to others, even in your desire to do what is good and to shun what is evil, that strength and courage may fail you at times, if you depend upon yourselves alone. In an army soldiers, especially young soldiers, are sometimes known to have been afraid. But there is one thing that nearly always stirs them to deeds of bravery and heroism. It is when they know that their commander is himself looking on. The eye of their general is upon them, and they do not think of, or they do not care for, dangers, obstacles, enemies ; on, on they go, under the eye of their commander, to win victory and glory that would otherwise have been impossible.

So may it be with you, dear children. Remember God's eye is upon you from the beginning of the year to the end of the year. Your Heavenly Commander will not fail you or forsake you. Remember God's words : " Have I not commanded thee ? Be strong and of a good courage ; be not afraid, neither be thou dismayed : for the Lord thy God is with thee, whithersoever thou goest."

RETURNING TO GOD

(*New West End Synagogue, Vestry Room,*
Day of Atonement, 1900.)

MALACHI iii. 7 : " Return unto Me, and I will return unto
you, saith the Lord of Hosts."

SOME children have a habit of straying and getting
themselves lost ? I have heard that, whenever a large
number of boys and girls go out for a day's holiday
together, one or two are sure to be missing when the
time comes for going home. How do they manage to
get lost ? Perhaps they see a pretty flower or a butter-
fly, and in order to get it, they begin by going just a
little way in another direction than that taken by the
rest. Then they go a little further in the wrong way,
and perhaps without knowing it take a wrong turning
and so lose themselves by degrees.

It is most unpleasant, is it not, to find yourself lost ?
You feel quite alone and deserted, and it seems as if
you can never get back home or find your friends again.
But after a time, if you are sensible, you begin to think.
You feel that you cannot have gone so very far after
all. You wait till you meet some one, and you tell him
where you live, and he will probably be kind enough
to offer to see you home. But before you have got very
far on your homeward way, what is most likely to happen ? You will see some one looking for you ; your

father or mother, or your elder brother or sister. They had not forgotten you, but they were looking for you all the time, and they are as glad to find you as you are to be found by them.

Now God is always looking for us, because we are always getting a little bit lost. He says : Do not go on getting farther and farther off ; come back to Me and I will come back to you. God is so anxious for us to go back to Him, that He meets us more than half way.

You, my dear children, have not very far to go to get back to God. Your little feet never carry you very far away from your parents and friends ; your little innocent hearts never take you very far from God. But I want to impress on you that you do sometimes wander a little away, and I want to make you understand that on this Day of Atonement you must try to get back nearer to the God who loves you, and wishes you always to keep as close to Him as you possibly can.

It is a great pity, but it is true, that we all find it hard to be always good. And being good *means* being close to God. When we are good we are near Him ; when we are bad we are far off. Hence, it is not easy for us to be always near to God, because it is not easy for us to be always good.

There is a beautiful story told by our wise men, which runs something to this effect :—When God was about to create man, He took into His counsel the angels that stood about His throne. " Create him not," said the Angel of Justice, " for if Thou dost, he will commit all kinds of wickedness against his fellow men ; he will be hard, and cruel, and dishonest, and unrighteous." " Create him not," said the Angel of Truth, " for he

will be false and deceitful to his brother man, and even
to Thee." " Create him not," said the Angel of Holiness ;
" he will follow that which is impure in Thy sight, and
dishonour Thee to Thy face." Then stepped forward
the Angel of Mercy, God's best beloved ; and Mercy said,
" Create him, O our Heavenly Father, for when he sins
and turns from the path of right and truth and holiness,
I will take him tenderly by the hand, and speak loving
words to him, and lead him back to Thee."

And God created man.

Ever since then, what the angels foresaw has come
to pass. Never has there been a sinless man. " There
is no man upon earth so righteous that he doeth only
good and sinneth not." Some have sinned grievously
indeed against the God who loves truth, and righteousness, and kindness, and humbleness, and holiness. And
all of us here gathered, even the youngest among us,
if they can think and remember at all, must feel that,
though God has given them the power to choose between
good and evil, they have often chosen the evil and
rejected the good. And yet, whatever be the evil we
have done and the good we have left undone, God's
mercy is ready to take us by the hand and help us to
be more true to ourselves and to Him. It is Mercy
that pleads for that forgiveness which we all need, great
and small, young and old.

Do you want an actual proof of what God's mercy
has done for us ? Why, the very Day of Atonement is
such a proof. It is a sign that God casts no one off,
however bad he may have been. It is a sign that,
though we have often forgotten Him, or ceased to care
for Him, He has not forgotten us, and never ceases to
care for us.

But the Day of Atonement, like other gifts and signs of God's love, must be properly used, if it is to do us any good. If there are any people foolish enough to think that God does everything for them on the Day of Atonement, and that they need do nothing for themselves, they are greatly mistaken. Do not you, dear children, spoil God's great blessing to you by any such folly. You might as well imagine that, when you are ill and the doctor comes to visit you, *that* is enough to make you well. If you do not follow the doctor's advice ; if you refuse to take his remedies ; if you say, I will eat and drink just what I like, though he tells me it is bad for me ; I will do all sorts of things according to my own fancy, though he warns me against them, you will find yourself worse off than before. Is it not absurd to suppose that a physician will help you by advice which you will not take ? God Himself, who is the great and loving Physician of all His children, will not cure us of sin (which is the sickness of the soul), spite of ourselves. We must meet Him, if He comes to meet us. That is what the prophet means when he says in God's name, " Return unto Me and I will return unto you." And on this holy day He is stretching out His hands to us—He is imploring us to come to Him, to confess our sins to Him, even as a sick person must tell the doctor all that ails him, to trust in Him, to follow Him, to love and obey Him. All day long He is saying to us, if we will but listen, " Return unto Me and I will return unto you."

You will remember that in the story I told you, there were three angels who objected to the creation of man. These were : the Angels of Justice, Truth, and Holiness. Have you, little children, done nothing against

these three virtues ?   Have you been just, truthful,
and holy ?

What does it mean to be *just* ?   It means many things,
but one thing will be enough to mention now.   Your
parents send you to school ; they sometimes spend
much money, they always spend much care on your
schooling.   Do you do your duty at school ?   Are you
attentive, well-behaved, anxious to do your best ?   If
not, you are unjust.   You are unjust to your parents
and your teachers.   Then are you fair to your school
friends ; are you always honourable, never doing a bad
turn, never taking an unfair advantage, never doing
a nasty, mean trick ?   If you fail in any of these directions you are unjust to your friends.   And you may
be unjust to yourselves.   For these injustices against
others are not only injustice against your own character, but if you even think mean thoughts then you
sin against your own innocence.   And, of course, you
are unjust to God.   He gave you a pure soul, and is
it just of you not to keep it clean ?   He tries to keep
you near, but you go away from Him.   Is that just ?
Then try to get back to God by the road of justice.

What does it mean to be *truthful* ?   You can answer
that question for yourselves.   You know how wicked
falsehood is.   Perhaps you will say you do not tell
any great untruths, and I believe you when you say
so.   But do you never tell *little* untruths ?   And you
can be untruthful without saying a word !   You can
deceive people by silence as well as by speech.   You
sometimes allow others to be punished for your fault,
and do not " own up."   Is that being truthful ?   You
sometimes persuade yourself that a lesson is too hard
for you, when in reality you are too lazy to do it.   Is

that being truthful ? You sometimes omit your morning prayers, and say, " O, I forgot." But is it always true that you forget ? Weren't you sometimes too idle, too indifferent, to say your prayers, though you very well remembered about it ? We often say : " I have no time," when we mean, " I have no will." All these are examples of untruthfulness, and you could, I am sure, tell me of many more if you liked. Of this be sure : every untruthful thought or act is a step taking you away from God. Then try to get back to God by the road of truth.

What does it mean to be *holy* ? It means to be pure, to have God in your thoughts and heart, to be religious and honest. And for you Jewish boys and girls it means something besides. God said that the people of Israel must be a holy nation. The Jews must not only be good, they must be *best*. The Jews must show the world that they belong to God, are very near to Him. Other people will learn to know and love God when they see that God's people are leading beautiful lives. Yet I have heard of Jewish boys in public schools who try not to be known as Jews at all ! If they are naughty boys, then I am glad if people do not know they are Jews. But if they are good boys, they will not only rejoice that they are Jews, but will try to make every one say : Judaism must be a wonderful religion if Jews are so good. Whenever people say the opposite—and I am sorry to say that the opposite often is said truly enough—then we defeat God's plan. He asked us to be the instrument by which the knowledge of Him should reach the world, but we are traitors to Him. You do not wish this to be said of you ? God wants you by your holy life to bring others near to Him ; will you by an unholy life drive them off from Him ? And not them only, but yourselves ; you, too, get farther from Him by such unholy example. So try to get back to God by the road of holiness.

But though I have called these " ways," they are all after all only byways ; they do but lead into the great highway, which goes straight to God—the highway of God's mercy.

This great, wide road of mercy is always open to you. That is God's highway, the way to Him. Be just, be truthful, be holy, and you have started right ; you are getting nearer to the great road back to your Father. He will help you to maintain your effort, He will hold out His hand to guide and support you.

God's love for you is so great that He would not have you spend a single day away from Him. He comes Himself, great and mighty as He is, and asks and entreats you to make your peace with Him. I suppose it has happened to every one of you, if you have done some wrong to anybody, that you have felt a desire to what is called " making it up." Now there are two reasons why you may be led to wish to " make it up." One is because you are suffering punishment, or are going to suffer it, and you dread being punished. You have fallen into disgrace, you are made to bear pain, you have to do without the pleasures which others have and you also would like to enjoy. In that case it is *fear* that drives you, and you want to make things right with those whom you have wronged or disobeyed because you are afraid of punishment—and so you repent. Well that kind of repentance is repentance from fear, and is not the best kind, and perhaps is not a *true* kind of repentance at all. But you might be impelled to "make it up" for another reason. Suppose the wrong you have done was done to some dear friend, to your own brother or sister, or to your own father and mother, who love you as no other human being loves you, in spite of all your faults; and suppose you knew that they were longing to forgive you, and actually offered you forgiveness for the asking, then I fancy you would say to yourselves, "I can't bear this any longer; I am ashamed of myself; I can't go on wounding the hearts that love me; I must make it up with them; their love has conquered my love." That would be repentance from *love*; that is the very best sort of repentance, if not the only true sort, and that sort of repentance rarely comes into any one's heart when he is no longer young. People, when they get older, very often feel sorry and grieved and unhappy after they have sinned, but their grief and sorrow and unhappiness is mostly for the dreadful consequences of their sin, for the suffering and sickness they bring upon themselves, or for their loss of money or of freedom, or for the disgrace that falls upon them and those who belong to them. But the good God wants us to be sorry for our *sins* far more than for the *consequences* of our sins, far more than for the punishment that follows upon our sins. Punishment indeed sooner or later always overtakes us for our sins—it may perhaps be a long time coming; Job was a very old man when he said, "Thou makest me suffer punishment for the sins of my youth" (xiii. 26). But if we are only sorry for the *punishment* and not for the *sin*, then we do not repent at all, and all the lessons of this holy day have been wasted upon us.

No sooner have you done an evil thing, an unjust,

or an untrue, or an unholy thing, than God's voice sounds in your heart—if you will but listen to it—and says, " Return unto Me and I will return unto you." Do not wait. *Do not be ashamed.* Ashamed to give up an evil habit ! Ashamed to do what is right ! Ashamed before your companions, and not ashamed before God ! What an awful thought that is ! Yes, do not wait until another Day of Atonement. Which of us knows whether he will live to see another Day of Atonement ? Have you not heard of men and women, of boys and girls, who were with us last year, but who have passed from this life since then ? And it is almost a certainty that some who are here to-day will be lost to this world next Yom Kippur. Do not wait an hour, a moment, but now at once listen to and answer God's call.

And answer it in this way ; stand up and repeat after me, sentence by sentence, these words :—Almighty and all merciful God ! Here am I, O Lord   speak Lord, for Thy servant heareth   I am yearning to make it up   with my Father in Heaven. I have done what Thou hast forbidden   I have left undone what Thou hast commanded.

I have done that   which makes me unworthy of Thy love. But without it   how dark and wretched must be my life. I cannot bear to think   that I have shut myself out   from Thy love. Teach me to know my duty better, in great things and in small   and to do it better   to everybody on Earth   and to Thee in Heaven. Come, Thou good and loving God   and help me   to find my way back to Thee.

Butler & Tanner, The Selwood Printing Works, Frome, and London.